30 PEOPLE
WHO CHANGED THE
WORLD

EDITED BY JEAN REYNOLDS

An iNK Nonfiction Minute Book

SEA
GRASS

First published in 2017 by Seagrass Press, an imprint of The Quarto Group.
6 Orchard Road, Suite 100, Lake Forest, CA 92630, USA.
T (949) 380-7510 F (949) 380-7575 www.QuartoKnows.com

Seagrass Press titles are also available at discount for retail, wholesale, promotional, and bulk purchase. For details, contact the Special Sales Manager by email at specialsales@quarto.com or by mail at The Quarto Group, Attn: Special Sales Manager, 401 Second Avenue North, Suite 310, Minneapolis, MN 55401 USA.

ISBN: 978-1-63322-377-6

Illustrations by Natasha Hellegouarch
Interior design by Marc Cheshire

MIX
Paper from responsible sources
FSC® C101537
www.fsc.org

Printed in China
10 9 8 7 6 5 4 3 2 1

CONTENTS

Introduction

BY JEAN REYNOLDS

Dear Readers,

You've just arrived at a party with a guest list of people who are guaranteed to be incredibly interesting. You will recognize some of the famous guests and know something about them, but there are others you don't recognize at all. They're an interesting crowd, obviously from different cultures and even different historical times.

- Check out the guy in the orange helmet who is carrying a strange-looking spear. You can have an in-depth chat with him about anything—astronomy, architecture, construction (pyramids are his specialty), poetry, philosophy, and medicine. If you enjoy the Marvel crime-fighting group S.H.I.E.L.D., bring that up. Even though he lived more than 4,000 years ago, he is credited as its founder.

- And what about the two ladies in the corner who look like they may be related? Each has such a regal look—one elderly and dressed totally in black, and the other young and beautiful, yet very familiar looking.

- You spot Julius Caesar and Albert Einstein at a glance. Everyone knows what they look like, but finding out more about them could be fun.

- You really want to learn more about the lady in the old-time pilot's helmet. Strange headgear for a lady with such elegant fingernails.

How do you fit into a party such as this? How do you find out enough about these fascinating guests to start a conversation?

You're in the right place. *30 People Who Changed the World: Fascinating Bite-Sized Essays from Award-Winning Writers* will tell you something about each of them. If it is someone you have never heard of, you may find out who she is and what she did (one of the guests you don't know invented the term "computer bug"). If you know the person, then interesting side stories will help you know him better. (Did you know that Julius Caesar was kidnapped by pirates and held for ransom?)

Your invitation to this party is compliments of some of the best children's nonfiction writers in the United States. They all got together to form an organization called iNK Think Tank. They created a blog called "The Nonfiction Minute" in order to interest, inspire, and entertain kids. This book is a collection of the biographies from that project.

Mingle and have a good time. What you learn while you're having fun could help *you* be a very interesting person, too—and perhaps even inspire you to change the world.

Enjoy every minute,

Jean Reynolds
Editor
The Nonfiction Minute
www.nonfictionminute.org

Marian Anderson

A Singer's Victory

BY AMY NATHAN

In 1963, at a ceremony in Washington, D.C., President Lyndon Johnson awarded singer Marian Anderson the Presidential Medal of Freedom, the highest honor a president can give to a civilian (someone not in the military). He explained why this African American musician was being honored: "Artist and citizen, she has ennobled her race and her country, while her voice has enthralled the world."

Twenty-four years earlier, however, some in Washington weren't interested in honoring her but instead treated her unfairly. By then, she had given wonderful concerts of classical music in Europe and the United States, including at the White House. But in 1939, when a local university tried to have her perform at Constitution Hall, Washington's concert hall, the managers of Constitution Hall wouldn't let her, just because of the color of her skin.

Eleanor Roosevelt, President Franklin Roosevelt's wife,

Portrait of Marian Anderson by photographer Carl Van Vechten.

7

Marian Anderson performs in front of 75,000 spectators in Potomac Park, Washington, D.C.

was upset by this example of discrimination against African Americans and arranged for Marian Anderson to perform that spring at the Lincoln Memorial. More than 75,000 people filled the area in front of the memorial to hear her sing. Thousands more around the country listened on radio to a live broadcast of the performance. She started by singing "America," then sang some classical pieces, and ended with spirituals, including "Nobody Knows the Trouble I've Seen." Newspapers and magazines wrote rave reviews, which let thousands more people learn about the dignified and courageous way she had triumphed over discrimination. Four years later, in 1943, she was at last invited to perform at Constitution Hall.

Did this end unfair treatment for this singer? Not

exactly. In 1953, Marian Anderson was again denied permission to perform at a concert hall, this time by the Lyric Theater in Baltimore, Maryland. Luckily, this city's music- and freedom-loving citizens came to her defense. Some wrote letters to newspapers complaining about "this insult to a great American singer."

Marian Anderson performing at the dedication of a mural installed in the United States Department of the Interior building in Washington, DC, commemorating the outdoor concert which she gave at the Lincoln Memorial.

Marian Anderson was the recipient of the Presidential Medal of Freedom awarded for "An especially meritorious contribution to the security or national interests of the United States, world peace, cultural or other significant public or private endeavors."

Others threatened never to go to that concert hall again. Hundreds complained directly to the Lyric's managers. Finally, Maryland's commission on interracial relations persuaded the Lyric's owners to let Marion Anderson perform there on January 8, 1954. The hall was filled to overflowing with her enthusiastic fans.

Ten years later, racial discrimination in concert halls finally became illegal. The Civil Rights Act of 1964 outlawed discrimination based on race, religion, or national origin at any place that serves the public, including concert halls, theaters, stadiums, restaurants, hotels, and anywhere else.

Find Out More

READ: *When Marian Sang: The True Recital of Marian Anderson* by Pam Munoz Ryan, illustrated by Brian Selznick

WATCH: Marian Anderson singing on the steps of the Lincoln Memorial: youtube.com/watch?v=mAONYTMf2pk

Thomas Boyle

The Superhero in a Supership Who Held Up Britain

BY JAN ADKINS

The Revolutionary War should have won the United States independence from Britain. Britain's Royal Navy didn't care. In the early 1800s it was busy fighting Napoleon, but it had time to stop United States merchant ships on the high seas from trading with France or British colonies. Britain always needed sailors, so its officers seized US sailors, claiming they were Royal Navy deserters.

The United States needed a more independent independence. President James Madison declared a second war against Britain in 1812. Britain declared an embargo, forbidding our ships to leave port.

A proclamation of blockade of the United Kingdom issued by Thomas Boyle, commander of the *Chasseur*, 1814.

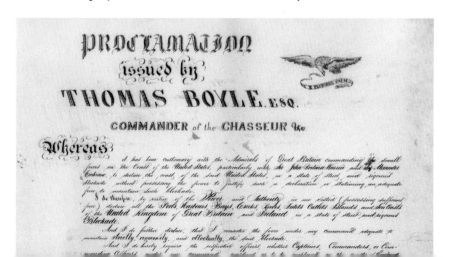

Portrait of Thomas Boyle by Jan Adkins

The Royal Navy had hundreds of big warships; the United States had six. To supplement its tiny Navy, the United States issued letters of marque, which are government licenses for privateers (private men o'war.)

The boldest and most successful privateer was Captain Thomas Boyle's *Chasseur*. It was a new kind of vessel, a Baltimore pilot schooner, the fastest ship afloat.

No sailboat can go directly into the wind. A square-rigged ship could manage to sail only 80 degrees to the left or right of the wind's direction. The *Chasseur* sailed 55 degrees off the wind. Working into the wind by tacking (sailing to one side of the wind, then the other) she could go 10 miles to windward by sailing about 24 miles on diagonal courses. The Royal Navy's square-rigged men o'war would log almost 59 miles to reach the same point.

Chasseur carried only 16 small cannons—no match for a big man o'war's 30 to 40 guns. But Boyle had no intention of slugging it out. If a man o'war appeared, he would scamper away to windward. *Chasseur* couldn't be caught.

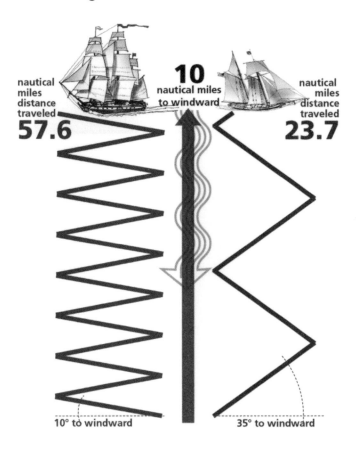

nautical miles distance traveled
57.6

10 nautical miles to windward

nautical miles distance traveled
23.7

10° to windward

35° to windward

Lithograph of the engagement between the American privateer *Chasseur* and HMS *St. Lawrence.*

Boyle crossed the Atlantic and quickly took 18 British merchant ships. He was bold as a lion: He sent the last vessel back into port, so its captain could nail a proclamation to the door of Lloyd's Coffee House, where London ship-insurers gathered. It was a politely worded embargo on all the British Isles—the same embargo Britain had attempted to force on the United States!

Did Boyle succeed? Yes and no. Many British ships sailed, but fear of the *Chasseur* raised the price of insurance by 300 percent! Some of Lloyd's insurers wouldn't write policies on ships voyaging near America. The US Navy was small but mighty: Its six heavy frigates (including Constitution, "Old Ironsides") beat many Royal Navy frigates ship-to-ship. The combination of daring, skill, and brass audacity won the War of 1812 against the largest navy in the world.

Find Out More

READ: *Pride of Baltimore: The Story of the Baltimore Clippers* by Thomas C. Gillmer

VISIT: pride2.org

Julius Caesar

A Man of His Word

BY JIM WHITING

When he was a young man in his mid-twenties, future Roman leader Julius Caesar was voyaging across the Mediterranean Sea. Pirates swarmed over his ship. They took him to their base on tiny Farmakonisi Island, which lies off the coast of Asia Minor (modern-day Turkey), and held him for ransom.

When he learned how much the pirates were demanding for his release, Caesar laughed. Do you have any idea who I am, he asked. I belong to one of Rome's most important families. So you can get more money for me—a lot more—almost three times as much. The astonished pirates were only too happy to oblige him.

Keeping a friend and two servants with him on Farmakonisi, Caesar ordered the rest of his traveling party to go to Asia Minor and raise his ransom. While they were doing that, Caesar acted as if he were the ruler of the tiny island, rather than a captive cowering in fright. He

A Roman coin depicting Julius Caesar, dating to the period 47 BCE to 46 BCE.

Marble bust of Julius Caesar.

ordered the pirates to attend lectures and poetry readings he gave, and prodded those who nodded off as he droned
on and on and on. When he wanted to sleep, he ordered the pirates to either speak in whispers or go to another part of the island. He even played games with them. He also told them that when he was released, I promise I will hunt you down and execute you. In the spirit of bonhomie he engendered, the pirates apparently thought he was joking.

Farmakonisi is a small Greek island in the chain of the Dodecanese islands in the Aegean Sea.

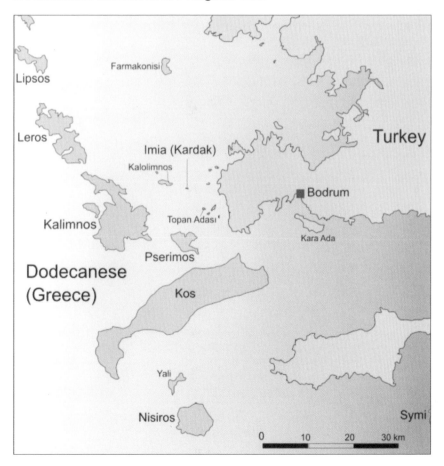

He wasn't. Though outwardly he was friendly with the pirates, he seethed inwardly at the humiliation of being taken prisoner. After the ransom was paid, Caesar sailed to a nearby port. He raised a fleet of ships and scores of armed men. He returned to Farmakonisi, captured the pirates, and reclaimed the ransom money. He threw his former captors into prison. They didn't stay there long. Caesar crucified them. He did show some mercy. Since crucifixion was a long, lingering death, he cut their throats so they died instantly.

Find Out More

READ: *The Life & Times of Julius Caesar* (Biography from Ancient Civilizations) by Jim Whiting

READ: "The Real Story Behind the Assassination of Julius Caesar," by Larry Getlin, nypost.com/2015/03/01/the-real-story-behind-the-assassination-of-julius-caesar

George Washington Carver

Sodbuster

BY CHERYL HARNESS

Did you know that George Washington Carver, the famous African American scientist, used to live in a little sod house on the prairie? Well, he did. And did you know that he built it himself? He did that, too, out in windy western Kansas.

Since he was 13 or so, Missouri-born George had been on his own. He did laundry to earn his keep while he lived in different families' spare rooms and went to any school that would accept a brilliant, curious, black boy. Such schools were hard to find in the early 1880s.

He applied to and got accepted to one Kansas college only to be turned away when the professors saw his dark skin. So he used his savings to buy some chickens and a half-mile square of land (160 acres) out near the tiny town of Beeler, Kansas, in the spring of 1886.

The Boy Carver statue, sculpted in 1960 by Robert Amendola, is at the George Washington Carver National Monument in Newton County, Missouri.

George Washington Carver after he earned his degree in agriculture.

His chickens were probably very happy with all the wiggly critters that appeared as 22-year-old George started sodbusting with tools he borrowed from his prairie neighbors. By that I mean he cut and dug up blocks of sod, which is topsoil plus grass roots. He lined up and stacked these heavy, earthen building blocks until he had his own soddy, a thick-walled sod cabin that was 14 feet square. Out on the prairies, there weren't many trees for wooden houses, but thin willows grew along the creeks. With willow poles, dry grass, and sod slabs, George could make a roof.

He planted little trees plus corn and other vegetables, and on Sundays, he went to church and sang hymns with his neighbors. George was very musical, with a fine tenor voice.

With their thick walls, soddies were cool in the summer and warm in the winter, but nobody was prepared for the winter that began in 1887. On January 12, 1888, the weather was balmy, but then the temperature dropped like an anvil, and a truly epic blizzard began. When the snow quit falling and the

A sod house. This one is probably much larger and more luxurious than the one young George built for himself.

George Washington Carver holding a piece of soil.

winds quit howling, nearly 500 people and thousands of cattle were frozen and dead out on America's Great Plains! George survived in his little cabin, but that was enough prairie life for him. He headed east, away from the frontier and, at last, got what he'd wanted all along: a proper education. George Washington Carver became the very first black graduate of the college known these days as Iowa State University.

Find Out More

READ: *The Groundbreaking, Chance-Taking Life of George Washington Carver and Science & Invention in America*, written and illustrated by Cheryl Harness

VISIT: shsmo.org/historicmissourians/name/c/carver/

VISIT: nps.gov/gwca/learn/historyculture/upload/1897-Or-Thereabouts-English-8-2010-final.pdf

Cesar Chavez

A Reluctant Hero

BY JIM WHITING

Before 1965, few Americans had heard of Delano, California, a town about 30 miles north of Bakersfield. At that time it had a population of just over 10,000. Its economy was centered on vast fields of vines that produced table grapes.

In the summer of 1965, growers actually cut the pay of the Filipino-Americans who harvested the grapes. On September 8, the workers responded with a strike against the growers. They wanted better pay and

Cesar Chavez (right) speaking at a 1974 United Farm Workers rally in Delano, California.

improved working conditions. The growers thought they could replace the Filipinos with Mexican field hands. It was a tactic that had worked in the past but things would be different this time.

This Filipino boy in a cauliflower field shows the hopeless discouragement of young field hands before collective bargaining was allowed.

The widespread farm workers grape boycott of 1965 stemmed from a labor rebellion for improved circumstances. Protest buttons were distributed in both English and Spanish.

Cesar Chavez—head of the predominantly Mexican National Farm Workers Association (soon renamed United Farm Workers)—reluctantly decided to join the strike. Born in 1927 in Arizona, Chavez had spent much of his early life experiencing life as a typical migrant worker—traveling with his family among a series of camps with wretched living facilities, dealing with racism, performing excruciatingly hard work in harsh direct sunlight for ridiculously low wages. He became involved in labor organizing when he was 25.

The town of Delano became ingrained into the national consciousness when Chavez assumed the leadership role in the strike. He adopted several tactics to advance his cause. He organized a 300-mile-plus march on the state capital of Sacramento to draw media attention. In the face of grower hostility, he emphasized nonviolence. He urged a nationwide boycott table of table grapes, and sent union members around the country to explain their position. He allied himself with the civil rights movement. He underwent a 25-day hunger strike.

The strike dragged on for nearly five years. Chavez and his followers persevered. Finally, on July 29, 1970, more than two dozen Delano growers signed contracts guaranteeing workers the right to unionize, thereby providing better pay and working conditions. The strike was over.

Chavez continued to work tirelessly on behalf of farm workers for the rest of his life. He even had an

This image is from a poster celebrating César Chávez Day which is observed in the U.S. on March 31 each year. It serves as a tribute to his commitment to social justice and respect for human dignity.

influence on the 2008 US presidential election. In 1972, he and his close associate Dolores Huerta coined the phrase *"Sí, se puede,"* which means "Yes, one can." It was a rallying cry for union members. President Barack Obama changed it slightly to "Yes, we can," and the slogan helped him rally his supporters.

Cesar Chavez died in 1993. Today California, Colorado, and Texas honor him with state holidays on March 31, his birthday.

Find Out More

READ: *Who Was Cesar Chavez?* by Dana M. Rau, illustrated by Ted Hammond and Nancy Harrison

VISIT: ufw.org/_page.php?inc=history/07.html

Bessie Coleman

The World's First Black Female Pilot

BY ROXIE MUNRO

Bessie Coleman, better known as Queen Bess, was America's first black woman pilot. She was born in Texas in 1892, into a world of extreme poverty and deepening racial discrimination. Her dream was to "amount to something one day." Bessie fought against

Bessie as a manicurist with high-flying dreams.

Bessie's daring training schedule included loop-the-loops.

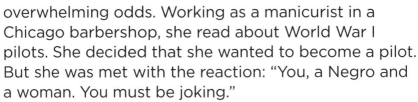

overwhelming odds. Working as a manicurist in a Chicago barbershop, she read about World War I pilots. She decided that she wanted to become a pilot. But she was met with the reaction: "You, a Negro and a woman. You must be joking."

Undeterred, Bessie sought the advice of a valued customer in the barbershop. "Go to France," he said. "The French are much more accepting of both women and blacks—but first learn the language."

That same day, Bessie began taking French lessons. A few months later, she sailed for France and signed

Bessie Coleman's French pilot's license

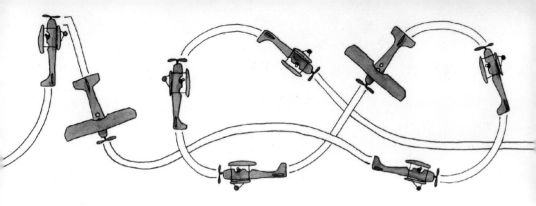

up with an aviation school. Her training included everything from banked turns and looping-the-loop to airplane maintenance. In 1921, she became the first black woman to earn a pilot's license.

Back in the United States, an African-American woman pilot was big news. Thunderous applause and a rousing rendition of "The Star-Spangled Banner" greeted Bessie at her first air show in New York. Memphis and Chicago followed. Bessie's future never looked brighter. She managed to buy an old Curtis Jenny, a favorite plane among barnstormers. She was heading for a performance in Los Angeles when the engine stalled; she crashed onto the street below, was knocked unconscious, broke one leg, and fractured several ribs.

Distraught over having disappointed her fans, she sent a telegram to the local newspaper: "AS SOON AS I CAN WALK, I'M GOING TO FLY!" Seven months later, she was back in a borrowed plane, performing to upbeat crowds in Ohio, Texas, and Florida.

Bessie loved flying and accepted its risks, but her real ambition was to open a flight school. Sadly, she didn't live to see her dream realized. In 1926, her old, run-down plane went into a spin. Bessie was thrown out of her seat and fell to her death.

At her funeral, thousands paid their respects to the brave young aviator. With her pluck and determination, Bessie Coleman had set an example for many black people.

Bessie flying over the countryside.

Shortly thereafter, the Bessie Coleman Aero Club in Los Angeles became a reality, introducing young blacks to the world of aviation. Among those inspired by Bessie was Dr. Mae Jemison, the first female African-American astronaut.

Find Out More

READ: *Feathers, Flaps, & Flops: Fabulous Early Fliers* by Bo Zaunders, illustrated by Roxie Munro

VISIT: pbs.org/wgbh/amex/flygirls/peopleevents/pandeAMEX02. html

Marie Curie

Science Was a Game

BY VICKI COBB

In October, 1891, 23-year-old Manya Sklowdowska arrived in Paris to attend the Sorbonne, France's great university. She had saved money, working as a governess to get there. She was determined to make the most of her studies in science and math. Right

Marie Curie, circa 1900.

Marie and Pierre Currie.

away she was noticed partly because she was Polish, although she had changed her first name to a French version, Marie, to fit in better. She always sat in the front row of all her classes because her French was not yet fluent and she didn't want to miss anything. She also was one of only a few female students. In a university full of smart people, she worked hard to excel. She ultimately finished first in her class and went on to make major scientific discoveries.

What made Marie so single-minded and determined? Behind it all was a great love for science, a love she shared with her husband, Pierre Curie, whom she met in 1894. At that time, science was uncovering unimaginable truths in chemistry and physics. New discoveries were being made at a breath-taking pace. Science was like a game and it attracted many players. Why?

1. There was a Nobel Prize for winners, those who discovered a big idea about the natural world. There was only one nature to discover, but people came at it from many directions.

2. It was collaborative. Scientists shared their discoveries by publishing papers.

3. It was competitive. The papers described procedures so that scientists could check each other's work. It kept everyone honest. The best work got the most attention.

4. The discoveries could be applied to solve problems for people. X-rays, light bulbs, phonographs, photographs, movies, and telephones would not have

Polish coin issued in 1967 celebrating the 100th anniversary of Marie Curie's birth.

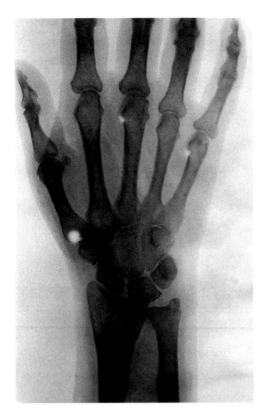

X-ray of a bullet wound to a hand.

been possible without science.

5. The biggest prize was the idea of the atom and its structure. Many scientists contributed to modern atomic theory, including Marie.

Marie Curie won the Nobel Prize twice for her work. At a time when women didn't even have the right to vote, she was a working mother of two daughters, a single mother after she was widowed in 1906, the founder of the Radium Institute for research, and she brought the X-ray to the battlefield in WWI. She believed that science could save the world, that scientific discoveries belonged to everyone. And she refused to benefit financially from her discoveries. Marie lived by the highest principles of honesty and integrity. She was a true champion of the science game.

Find Out More

READ: *Marie Curie: A Photographic Story of a Life* by Vicki Cobb

VISIT: smithsonianmag.com/history/madame-curies-passion-74183598/

Juan de Pareja

The Painter Was a Slave

BY SARA ALBEE

Diego Velázquez (1599–1660) was a famous Spanish painter. He had a slave named Juan de Pareja (1606–1670). Call him an indentured servant if you want, but it's more accurate to say he was Velázquez's slave, as he was not at liberty to leave. For years, Pareja

Diego Velázquez, *Portrait of Juan de Pareja*, 1650, Oil on Canvas, Metropolitan Museum of Art, New York.

prepared brushes, ground pigments, and stretched canvasses for the artist. While he was at it, De Pareja observed his master carefully, and secretly taught himself how to use the materials and how to paint.

Pareja was referred to as a Morisco in Spanish. One way to translate the word is that he had mixed parentage (the offspring of a European Spaniard and a person of African descent). Another way to translate the word is that he was a Moor—someone descended

Left: Juan de Pareja, *The Calling of Saint Matthew,* Oil on Canvas (Museo del Prado, 1661)

Below: Juan de Pareja, *Portrait of a Monk,* Oil on Canvas (State Hermitage Museum, 1651)

from Muslims who had remained in Spain after its conquest by Ferdinand and Isabella.

In 1650, Velázquez was preparing to paint a portrait of Pope Innocent X. As practice, he painted De Pareja, who had accompanied the artist to Italy. That portrait, shown on page 35, is pretty amazing, isn't it?

Velázquez got all sorts of praise for it from the artists in Rome. He was even elected into the Academy of St. Luke.

According to some sources, Velázquez would not allow De Pareja to pick up a paintbrush. But one day, when King Philip IV was due to visit Velázquez, De Pareja placed one of his own paintings where the king would see it. When the king admired it, believing it to be by Velázquez, De Pareja threw himself at the king's feet and begged for the King to intercede for him. Whether or not that story is true, De Pareja did become an accomplished painter, and impressed the king so much that he ordered De Pareja freed.

De Pareja remained with the Velázquez family until his death.

Find Out More

READ: *I, Juan de Pareja* by Elizabeth Borton de Treviño. (Newbery Medal Award winner, 1966)

VISIT: metmuseum.org/art/collection/search/437869

Charles Dickens

How His Story *A Christmas Carol* Helped the Poor

BY ANDREA WARREN

In 1843, thirty-one-year-old Charles Dickens had money problems. His wife was expecting their sixth child, he was in debt, and he supported a slew of needy relatives. He was known for writing long novels that were published in weekly installments, but because time was of the essence, he decided to write a short story that he could publish quickly. It was actually a long story by our standards but short by his.

The British were enamored with the paranormal, so he decided it would be a ghost story. To increase interest, he included three ghosts. And to seal the deal, he added a bonus apparition that appeared at the stroke of midnight, dragging its chains from hell. That would get readers' attention.

He didn't intend to simply entertain them. He was Charles Dickens, after all,

Charles Dickens, circa 1867-68.

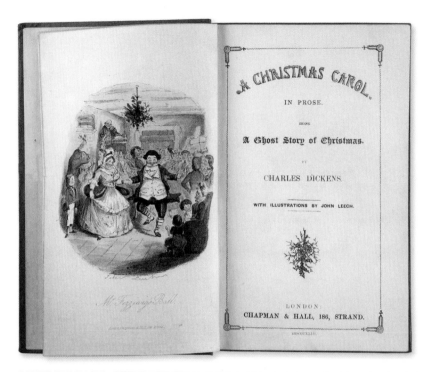

The title page of the original 1843 edition of *A Christmas Carol*, illustrated by John Leech.

and his writing was also meant to inspire. His family had once been poor, and his quest, as always, was to help the less fortunate. The tale he crafted happened at Christmas, a holiday that in England included charitable giving—the perfect setting for his messages that charity must come from the heart, and that it's never too late for redemption.

From his fertile imagination, he conjured up Ebenezer Scrooge, "a squeezing, wrenching, grasping, clutching, covetous, old sinner!" whose refrain to anything distasteful was "Bah, humbug!" Scrooge represented the self-serving upper classes, while his poorly paid clerk, Bob Cratchit, and his family, including sickly Tiny Tim, represent the deserving poor.

Dickens sent Scrooge on a wild night's journey, led by the ghosts of Christmases past, present, and future. Scrooge visited his childhood and learned why he'd become such a miserable miser, and he saw a grim future awaiting him if he didn't change his ways. By sunrise on Christmas morning, he was a new man. His hard heart had melted, and he became a good friend to the poor, beginning with the Cratchit family. He resolved to "honor Christmas in my heart, and try to keep it all the year."

To Dickens' delight, his readers did the same. In example after example, *A Christmas Carol* inspired

Marley's Ghost by John Leech.

Scrooge's Third Visitor (above) and *The Last of the Spirits* (right) by John Leech.

the upper classes to be more charitable to the lower classes. And because the book became a bestseller, it eased Dickens' financial worries.

Dickens' ghost story remains popular today, reminding us all that it's never too late to do the right thing, and allowing us to proclaim with Tiny Tim, "God bless us, every one!"

Find Out More

READ: *A Christmas Carol* by Charles Dickens

READ: *Charles Dickens and the Street Children of London* by Andrea Warren

Albert Einstein in 1921.

Albert Einstein

How His Shifting Nature of Space and Time Made Twins Become Not-So-Twins

BY JAN ADKINS

Albert Einstein's work wasn't done in a laboratory but in his marvelous mind, and he thought big. His thoughts about enormous speeds and giant masses changed the way we think of science and nature.

Einstein established a new approach to science: relativity, in which the mass and speed of objects are stable only in relation to their surroundings. One

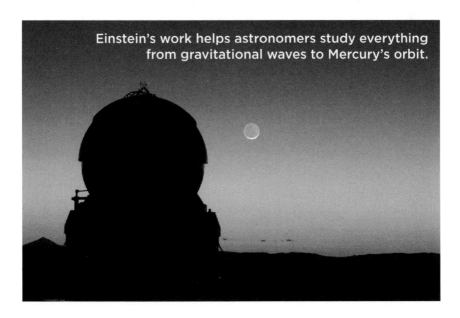

Einstein's work helps astronomers study everything from gravitational waves to Mercury's orbit.

Twins Bill and Will before their departure.

inescapable part of relativity is that space and time are parts of the same fabric. Very big masses and very fast speeds can warp that fabric.

One surprise discovery: There is a limit to how fast anything may travel. Anything approaching the speed of light requires more and more energy to push it only a little closer, until it can't be pushed more. Unless we solve this problem, c (the symbol for the speed of light) is as fast as we're going to get. But if you travel close to c, unusual things happen.

Bill, the traveling twin, is now 49, thanks to a round trip to Alpha Centauri. Will, the Earthbound twin, is 69.

Two twins, Bill and Will, plan to make a fast trip to the nearest star, Alpha Centauri, on their twentieth birthday. The distance is about four light-years away from Earth (light-year = distance light travels in a vacuum in one year, about 5,865,696,000,000 miles). Will is stuck in a traffic jam and misses the blast off. Bill goes alone. He travels very close to the speed of light (.9999999 c), whips around Alpha Centauri, and returns at the same speed. When he lands he asks for his brother Will.

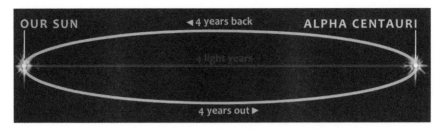

OUR SUN   ◄ 4 years back   ALPHA CENTAURI

4 light years

4 years out ►

Bill's travel map.

Bill has been traveling for a bit over eight years; he's 28 years old. But at this speed, his spaceship time has played out sloooooowly in relation to earth time. To Will on Earth, Bill's trip took 49 years. Will is now 69 years old.

If the spaceship had traveled a little bit faster, say .99999999 c, Bill would still have aged 8 years. But when he returned to Earth, Will and everyone else he knew would be dead, since 155 years would have passed.

Recently, with fantastically accurate clocks, we've proved Einstein's theories: Astronauts traveling at thousands of miles an hour on space stations age a few seconds slower for every year of Earth-time.

Can we ever travel to distant stars? Not unless we find a way around Einstein's shifting nature of space and time. Easy for *Star Trek*. So far, it's impossible for us.

Find Out More

READ: *Albert Einstein and Relativity for Kids: His Life and Ideas with 21 Activities and Thought Experiments* by Jerome Pollen

VISIT: trendingsideways.com/index.php/the-theory-of-relativity-for-kids-part-2-the-twin-paradox/

VISIT: gizmodo.com/5765603/this-animated-video-simplifies-einsteins-complicated-twin-paradox

Sarah Keys Evans

An Early Pioneer for Justice

BY AMY NATHAN

Rosa Parks is famous for refusing to move to the back of a bus in Montgomery, Alabama, in 1955. Buses were segregated there, with rules that made African Americans sit in the back. However, Rosa Parks wasn't the first to protest against such unfair bus rules. Others had done so earlier, including Sarah Keys Evans, a young private in the United States Army who made her stand for justice three years before Rosa Parks.

In August 1952, Sarah was traveling home to North Carolina from Ft. Dix in New Jersey, where she was stationed. Early that summer morning, she boarded a bus in New Jersey—where buses weren't segregated—and sat

A December 3, 1955 article from the *New York Age*—one of the most influential African American newspapers of its time.

ICC Ruling On Travel 'Frees' Brooklyn Girl

Sarah Keys, the ex-Wac now living in Brooklyn who waged a three-year successful battle to get segregation banned in interstate travel, because she felt it was a matter of moral decency, told the she "felt free" at long last.

"I've never been so happy in my life," she continued. "This is just the greatest thing for me and my people. It's a wonderful thing for the whole American people as well."

The Interstate Commerce Commission ruled that segregation of passengers in interstate travel on railroads or buses is unlawful, knocking out the separate but equal policy in vogue since 1887.

3-YR. CASE

In another ruling in the suit brought by the NAACP against 12 southern railroads, the ICC also banned segregation in train and bus waiting rooms.

Sarah Keys case began in Au-

See FREED, Page 6

SARAH KEYES

49

Sarah Louise Keys (before she married Evans) in uniform.

toward the middle of the bus. After midnight, the bus
entered Roanoke Rapids, a town in North Carolina.
Sarah's hometown was farther south. A new bus
driver took over the bus and ordered her to move to
the back. When she didn't, she was arrested. She had
to spend the night in jail and pay a $25 fine the next

morning. Police put her on another bus that took her the rest of the way home, forcing her to sit in the back.

With the help of a young African American lawyer, Dovey Roundtree, Sarah Keys Evans filed a complaint against the bus company with the Interstate Commerce Commission (ICC). Sarah won!

The ICC was in charge of interstate transportation— buses and trains that travel from state to state. The ICC said it was wrong for interstate buses to force people to sit in certain seats because of their race. This victory was announced one week before Rosa Parks

Sarah Louise Keys Evans is now 85 and lives in Brooklyn, New York.

The Women in Military Service for America Memorial in Washington, D.C.

made her stand on a different kind of bus—a local city bus, not an interstate one. Rosa Parks' action led to a year-long protest in Montgomery and a Supreme Court victory that called for an end to segregation on local buses, too. It would take several years, however, and more protests before both of these rulings were finally obeyed in all parts of the country.

In recent years, Sarah Keys Evans has received several important honors, including an award from the U.S. Department of Justice, a proclamation from Congress, and a plaque at the Women's Memorial in Washington. She was also honored in the place where her troubles began. An exhibit about her role in civil rights history was installed in the town museum of Roanoke Rapids, North Carolina.

Find Out More

READ: *Take a Seat—Make a Stand* by Amy Nathan

VISIT: army.mil/article/120456

Frederick Grant

A Boy Goes to War

BY ANDREA WARREN

Would parents willingly send their twelve-year-old son to war? During the U.S. Civil War, that's exactly what General Ulysses Grant and his wife, Julia, did. Of course they expected Frederick to stay safely behind Union lines—only Frederick wasn't the type to miss any excitement, and he ended up paying a big price for that.

Ulysses S. Grant, wife Julia, and their children Frederick (standing), Buck, Nellie, and Jesse.

Frederick (seated, fourth from left in the oval), with his father (standing in the middle) and his officers.

It wasn't unusual for officers to have a family member with them, for they often faced separations that could last months or even years. Grant knew the campaign to silence Confederate cannons along the Vicksburg, Mississippi waterfront that were preventing Union ships from taking control of the Mississippi River was going to be a long one. He was a devoted family man and became depressed if away from his wife and four children for very long. Julia suggested their eldest son keep Grant company. Frederick, who wanted to make the military his career, was thrilled.

I learned about Frederick while researching my book *Under Siege! Three Children at the Civil War Battle for Vicksburg*. He joined a boy and girl who were inside Vicksburg as my eye-witnesses to Grant's brutal forty-seven-day siege in 1863 of that little river town.

And what an eye-witness he was! As the general's son, he had his own uniform and pony. He accompanied Grant during daily troop inspections and shared his tent at night. He knew he was supposed to stay in camp, but he was so eager to be part of the action, and several times he put himself in harm's way. That ended when he foolishly rode into battle only to be shot in the leg by a Confederate sniper. Frederick realized that if his leg were to be amputated—common treatment for a bullet wound—he'd never be a soldier. Even though his leg became painfully infected, doctors were able to save it. But in his weakened condition, he became ill with typhoid fever, a common camp disease.

Detail from a chromolithograph print decpicting the Siege of Vicksburg.

General Frederick Grant and his wife, Ida, in 1905.

He was still recuperating in his father's tent when Grant received word of Vicksburg's surrender. Frederick limped outside to excitedly announce the Union's victory to the troops.

Luckily, Frederick fully recovered. He returned to school and later served as his father's private secretary while Grant was President of the United States. He also joined the army, rising to the rank of general. The siege of Vicksburg had taught him a hard lesson about what it took to be a military man.

Find Out More

READ: *Three Children at the Civil War Battle for Vicksburg* by Andrea Warren.

VISIT: americancivilwarphotos.com/category/battles/battle-vicksburg

George Frederic Handel

Using Music to Help British Orphans

BY ANDREA WARREN

One of the joys of research is uncovering the unexpected. Most recently this happened to me when I was writing *Charles Dickens and the Street Children of London*. Dickens was a patron of the London Foundling Hospital, a charitable home for orphans

The Foundling Hospital in 1753.

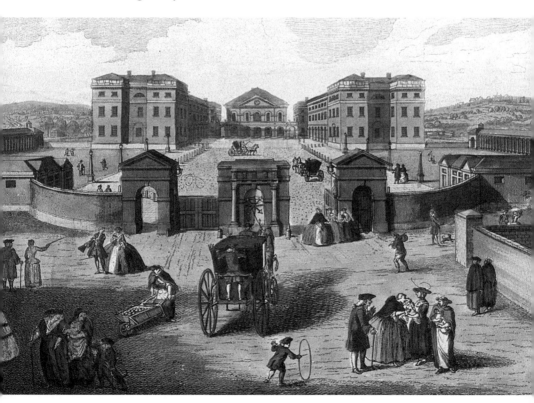

established in 1741. (Foundlings were children whose parents were unknown, and hospital meant shelter back then.)

Researching the Foundling, I learned that a century before Dickens, German composer George Frederic Handel was one of its greatest benefactors. I thought this must be a mistake since he was German. Curious, I took a side journey into Handel's life to find out.

Brimming with musical talent, Handel moved to London at age 26 to find work and quickly became a popular composer and performer. He decided to stay, eventually becoming a British citizen. Londoners readily recognized him for he was a great bear of a man who spoke with a thick German accent, and when angry, his

Handel embraced his new life in London with enthusiasm. He wore an enormous wig and very stylish clothes.

The chapel of the London's Foundling Hospital, the venue for regular charity performances of *Messiah* from 1750.

words tumbled together in German, Italian, and English. He never married or had children, but he had a big heart and readily assisted the needy and destitute, especially children. It's been said that no other composer contributed so much to the relief of human suffering.

He often helped charities by donating all proceeds from a concert. In 1749 when he learned that the Foundling did not have funds for its proposed chapel, he offered a concert to introduce his newest composition, *Messiah*. The packed audience was enthralled. A second concert quickly sold out, and the chapel was completed.

Handel became a member of the Foundling's Board of Governors and continued his financial assistance by personally directing *Messiah* in the chapel at least once

The cover page for the sheet music of *Messiah.*

a year, always to overflowing crowds. When the king attended a performance, he stood for the "Hallelujah Chorus," and audiences have been standing ever since. Because Handel knew people would pay to see it, he willed the Foundling an original copy of *Messiah.*

I listen to Handel's compositions differently now. It's no longer mere music from the past; instead, it feels alive, created by a fascinating man with a charitable heart who helped provide for orphans. I attend Messiah whenever I can, and when we all stand for the "Hallelujah Chorus," I smile to myself, feeling a strong connection to history, for I know exactly why we are doing it.

Find Out More

WATCH: youtube.com/watch?v=C3TUWUyg4s&index=10&list= RDVI6dsMeABpU.

READ: *Charles Dickens and the Street Children of London* by Andrea Warren

Grace Hopper

The Admiral in Command of Knowledge

BY JAN ADKINS

She was 15 pounds below minimum weight for the Navy when she joined, but she had a mighty mind. Admiral Grace Hopper changed the Navy. And your world.

She graduated from Vassar College in math and physics then earned a doctorate from Yale in math. She joined the Navy in World War II because it needed mathematicians to build the massive machines that computed tables of distance, gun elevation, projectile weight, windage, and other factors for precise naval gunnery. Almost immediately, she saw something other mathematicians didn't see: computers could talk.

They weren't just number crunchers to Grace. They could do much, much more if they were given a simple language that would bring

Commodore Grace M. Hopper, January 1984.

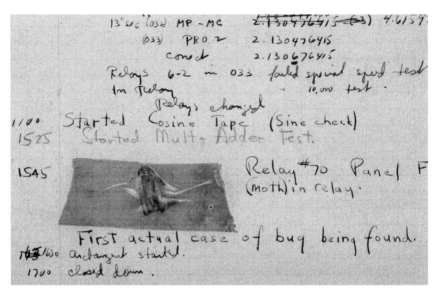

13"sec (032) MP -MC   2.130477675 (-3) 4.6159
(033)   PRO.2   2.13047645
conect   2.13067645

Relays 6-2 in 033 failed special speed test
in Relay   10.000 test .

Relays changed

1100   Started Cosine Tape (Sine check)
1525   Started Multt Adder Test.

1545   Relay #70 Panel F
                                          (moth) in relay.

First actual case of bug being found.
1630 antangent started.
1700 closed down .

While Grace Hopper was working on a Mark II Computer at a US Navy research lab in Dahlgren, Virginia in 1947, her associates discovered a moth stuck in a relay and thereby impeding operation. When they removed the moth, she remarked that they were "debugging" the system. Here is the famous bug. If you want a closer look at this famous bug, its remains can be found in the group's log book at the Smithsonian Institution's National Museum of American History in Washington, D.C.

the advantages of gigantic computing power and enormous data storage to common uses.

While working on the early computers she developed a "compiler," a kind of translating machine that turned plain-language needs into a set of mathematical commands that retrieved number data from storage banks, performed thousands or millions of math operations, and provided real-world answers.

In 1959 she was crucial in devising the first broad-based computer language, COBOL (COmmon Business Oriented Language). It is the root of the many computer operating systems we use today.

Then-Captain Grace worked with the National Bureau of Standards to develop self-testing capabilities so a computer could "de-bug" itself. She coined this word when she extracted a fried moth disrupting one of her computers.

She led the Navy away from a few giant computers to interconnected, smaller, scattered computers, opening the door to the Internet.

In 1985, at 79, she was promoted to rear admiral of the United States Navy Reserve. She said, "The most important thing I've accomplished, other than building the compiler, is training young people. They come to me, you know, and say, 'Do you think we can do this?' I say, 'Try it.' And I back 'em up. They need that. I keep

Secretary of the Navy, John Lehman, right, promotes Capt. Grace Hopper to the rank of commodore in a 1983 ceremony at the White House. President Ronald Reagan is at the left.

The guided-missile destroyer USS Hopper (DDG-70).

track of them as they get older and I stir 'em up at intervals so they don't forget to take chances." She died in 1992 at 85.

Admiral Grace Hopper received many awards and decorations but the Navy's most sincere tribute came in 1996 when it named the guided missile cruiser DDG-70, USS *Hopper*. Naturally, its sailors call their ship "Amazing Grace."

Find Out More

READ: *The Girl Who Could Talk to Computers - An Inspirational Tale About Grace Hopper* by Maya Cointreau

READ: *Mathematician and Computer Scientist Grace Hopper* by Andrea Pelleschi

VISIT: kidscodecs.com/grace-hopper

Imhotep

A Renaissance Man—4,000 Years Before the Renaissance

BY JIM WHITING

The Renaissance began in Europe in the 15th century and marked the change from the Medieval Period to the modern world. Towering figures, such as Michelangelo, Galileo, and especially Leonardo da Vinci, were known as Renaissance men because of their talents and lasting achievements in several important areas of knowledge. They were also accomplished musicians, public speakers, athletes, poets, and so forth. And they were expected to do all this stuff without breaking a sweat.

You could give the same title to an ancient Egyptian named Imhotep, who lived about 2600 BCE. He was the vizier (the most important government official) during the reign of Pharaoh Djoser. He served as the high priest of the god Ra and was an expert astronomer.

Imhotep designed and oversaw the building of the first major pyramid in Egypt. Located at

Statuette of Imhotep at the Louvre Museum.

Egyptologists ascribe to Imhotep the design of the Pyramid of Djoser (the Step Pyramid) at Saqqara in Egypt in 2630–2611 BCE.

Saqqara, it was the world's tallest structure at the time. He innovated the use of stones rather than mud bricks to build it, and it was that added strength that enabled the pyramid to rise so high. He is also credited with the invention of several devices that facilitated the construction.

Many people believe that Imhotep, rather than the Greek Hippocrates who lived more than 2,000 years later, is the real "Father of Medicine." In an era when most physicians relied on magic spells and appeals to the gods, Imhotep prescribed dozens of effective down-to-earth treatments for illnesses and injuries.

He is credited with ending a seven-year famine in Egypt. He advised the pharaoh to make sacrifices to Khnum, the god of the annual flooding of the Nile River, and thereby provide desperately needed water to farmers. On a more practical level, he invented an improved irrigation system to carry water to the crops even if the river level was abnormally low.

Bronze statuette of Imhotep with gold inlay made in Egypt between the 5th and 1st century BCE.

Imhotep is believed to be the original author of the content of the Edwin-Smith Papyrus, the earliest known writing on medicine.

In addition to these accomplishments, an inscription at the base of one of his statues notes that he was "Chief Carpenter, Chief Sculptor, and Maker of Vases in Chief." In his little spare time, he wrote poetry and dispensed philosophical advice.

Imhotep can also boast of two accomplishments that eluded even Leonardo da Vinci. He was deified after his death and worshipped for many centuries, an honor accorded to hardly anyone besides the pharaohs. And today the comic book community gives him the credit for founding S.H.I.E.L.D., the Marvel Comics espionage and crime-fighting agency that became the basis for blockbuster movies such as *Iron Man*, *Thor*, and *Captain America*.

Find Out More

VISIT: ancient-egypt-online.com/imhotep.html

Percy Julian

Creative Chemist

BY KERRIE LOGAN HOLLIHAN

Percy Julian was my neighbor in Oak Park, Illinois. I didn't know the family who lived in the pretty home surrounded by an iron fence. But I heard the story, that the house was firebombed after they had bought it back in 1951. The Julians were African-Americans coming to a white community.

Later I learned more. Dr. Julian was someone who didn't take no for an answer. He grew up in the segregated South going to black-only schools. He hoped to study plant chemistry, but no Southern college would accept a Negro, so he moved on. He went to DePauw University in Indiana and helped pay tuition by waiting tables at a white fraternity. He graduated at the top of his class in 1920 and wanted to pursue his doctorate at Harvard. Harvard refused because that would mean Julian could teach whites—and that was not allowed.

Julian moved on. He went to Austria to earn his doctorate, and in that lab, he studied

A gifted student, Percy Julian graduated from DePauw University in 1920.

Although he was discouraged from pursuing a career in chemistry and faced racist resistance, Percy Julian ignored the naysayers and broke new ground in his field.

chemicals in plants, especially beans. Many excellent medicines came from plant chemicals, but extracting them was often costly.

Upon returning to DePauw to teach, Julian was able to synthesize a plant chemical called physostigmine. His discovery produced inexpensive medicine for patients with glaucoma, an eye disease causing blindness. But the Great Depression fell across America, and DePauw ran out of money to fund his research.

Julian moved on. A Chicago paint company hired Julian as the first African-American to head a research lab in American industry. Julian had to travel for his work, and motels refused him a bed. One year he slept in his car 32 times, sometimes in the dead of winter.

In 1933 Julian accepted an appointment as a research fellow at DePauw University, where he directed research projects for senior chemistry majors.

This Percy Julian stamp was issued in 1993 to commemorate Black History Month.

Julian and his coworkers developed inks and paper coatings, dog food, and a product called Aero-Foam to extinguish fires on aircraft carriers. His team discovered many uses for soybeans, at that time viewed as food for cows and pigs. Most importantly, they synthesized "Substance S" from soybeans. This synthetic drug replaced wildly expensive cortisone. Julian's landmark achievement offered relief to kids suffering from the painful and disfiguring disease rheumatoid arthritis.

Percy Julian worked all his days, always moving on to make life better. He built his own research business, volunteered at church, played the piano, and loved his family. He became a quiet hero to many, including me. I'm writing a book about Dr. Julian, which I hope you'll see in print.

Find Out More

VISIT: chemheritage.org/percy-julian/activities/11a.html

Mary Kingsley

One Spunky Lady

BY ROXIE MUNRO

"It is at these times you realize the blessing of a good, thick skirt," said Mary Kingsley after she crashed into a cleverly concealed leopard pit lined with twelve-inch ivory spikes.

The year was 1895, the place Equatorial West Africa, and the spunky lady saved, thanks to her observance to the dress code of the day, was a young

"It is at these times you realize the blessing of a good, thick skirt."

Englishwoman collecting species of fish and beetles for the British Museum.

Mary Kingsley was the daughter of a physician who spent most of his time traveling. Although she received no formal education (which was reserved for her brother Charles), Mary learned to read, becoming fascinated with subjects such as science, exploration, and piracy.

At one point, she was granted permission to teach herself German, but only after she could iron a shirt properly. Mary learned chemistry, experimented with gunpowder and electricity, and became engrossed by the intricacies of plumbing. After years of caring for her invalid mother, in 1892 both her parents died. With the small inheritance left to her came the fulfillment of a dream: to explore West Africa.

Nothing like a "clip on the snout" to ward off an ill-tempered crocodile.

"Indeed, much as I have enjoyed life in Africa, I do not think I ever enjoyed it to the full as I did when dropping down the Rembwe... Ah me! Give me a West African river and a canoe for sheer pleasure."

When Mary crashed into the leopard pit, she was traveling in what was then the French Congo, getting to know the Fangs, reportedly a tribe of cannibals. Traveling by canoe, she was once marooned in a crocodile-infested lagoon. When one tried to climb aboard, she was there with a paddle, ready to "fetch him a clip on the snout."

After two trips, she wrote a book called *Travels in West Africa*. She became a sought-after lecturer and celebrity. In public appearances, she was both funny

Photo of Mary Kingsley from her book *Travels in West Africa* (1897).

and serious, peppering her narrative with jokes, often at her own expense, but also being critical of the way the British had steamrolled into the African continent, with little regard for its ancient cultures.

In 1900 she sailed to Africa for the third time, responding to an urgent call for nurses in South Africa, where war was underway. Assigned to a hospital where hundreds of soldiers were dying from a raging epidemic, she became ill herself, and died two months later. She was buried at sea with military honor.

In her book, she remembers: "Indeed, much as I have enjoyed life in Africa, I do not think I ever enjoyed it to the full as I did when dropping down the Rembwe... Ah me! Give me a West African river and a canoe for sheer pleasure."

Find Out More

READ: *Crocodiles, Camels & Dugout Canoes: Eight Adventurous Episodes* by Bo Zaunders, illustrated by Roxie Munro

VISIT: womenineuropeanhistory.org/index.php?title=Mary_Kingsley

Lafayette and Armistead

The Aristocrat and the Spy

BY CHERYL HARNESS

Since 1775, Americans in the thirteen British colonies had been fighting to free themselves from mighty Great Britain. The French didn't care for the British, having had their own wars with them, so many a Frenchman came to help the Americans. One was a teenaged aristocrat, the Marquis de Lafayette. He

Portrait of James Armistead Lafayette from a facsimile of the Marquis de Lafayette's original certificate commending Armistead for his revolutionary war service.

Marquis de Lafayette as a lieutenant general, in 1791. Portrait by Joseph-Désiré Court.

so admired America's revolutionary ideals of liberty and democracy that he sailed there in 1777 to offer his money and services to his idol, General George Washington. By 1781, General Lafayette was leading French and American troops, battling the British in Virginia. A fellow there named James Armistead joined the fight, once he got his master's permission. After all, Armistead was an enslaved African American.

What did he do? He hung around the British, finding out what they were up to—dangerous work! Then Armistead, patriot spy, took his info to General Lafayette, who used it to help beat the British at Yorktown in October 1781, which in turn, led to the United States' victory in the Revolutionary War.

The Marquis went back to France. Armistead went back to work for his master. Although he'd helped win America's independence, he did not win his. When Lafayette made a return visit in 1784, he was outraged to find his fellow veteran still enslaved! The Marquis saw to it that Armistead was freed, and the former slave showed his gratitude by changing his name to James Armistead Lafayette.

But this isn't how the story ends. Forty years later, the Americans invited the Marquis to come for a visit. He'd

The Surrender of Lord Cornwallis by John Trumbull.

Medallion commemorating Lafayette's tour of America in 1824–1825.

grown old. He'd suffered in prison during France's own revolution in the 1790s. How splendid it was, visiting the United States—all 24 of them! Oh, the parties and banquets the Americans had for their old friend! But one of the happiest moments of all was in early 1825. The old aristocrat was riding in a parade through Richmond, Virginia, when he spotted a white-haired black gentleman in the crowd. The Marquis reined in his horse, dismounted, and went to greet James Armistead Lafayette. And the two old heroes of the American Revolution flung their arms around one another.

Find Out More

READ: *A Spy Called James: The True Story of James Lafayette, Revolutionary War Double Agent* by Anne Rockwell, illustrated by Floyd Cooper

VISIT: army.mil/article/119280/James_Arimistead_Lafayette

Edmonia Lewis

A Sculptor Full of Surprises

BY CHERYL HARNESS

Every year, many thousands of people visiting Washington DC make their way to the crossing of 8th and F Streets to an *enormous* building with many columns. Once it was the US Patent Office Building. Now it's the Smithsonian American Art Museum. And there, up on the third floor, those visitors might well admire a big statue of Egypt's Cleopatra VII, at the moment when she was dying in the summer of 30 B.C. She was carved in Italy, out of snow-white marble.

When people first saw it in Philadelphia in 1876 at America's big 100th birthday party, they were so surprised to discover that the sculptor was a woman! Still more unusual, she was an African American. Her name was Mary Edmonia Lewis.

Patent Office Building, 1875.

Left: A photograph of Edmonia Lewis. Right: Edmonia Lewis, *The Death of Cleopatra,* Marble (Smithsonian American Art Museum, 1876)

Her ancestors came from Africa, Haiti, and the Native American Ojibwa (or Chippewa) tribe. She grew up in western New York. With money her big brother made mining for gold out West, talented Edmonia went to Ohio's Oberlin College, but not for long. Two white girls there lied, saying she tried to poison them, then a bunch of people beat her up. So her brother helped her settle in Boston, where she learned to sculpt. By age 20, Ms. Lewis had her own sculpture studio. She was so successful that she was able to leave racist, Civil War–torn America in 1865 to sculpt and study in Rome. When she heard the glorious news that the war was over and America's slaves were emancipated, she celebrated by sculpting an African American man and woman unchained.

Edmonia Lewis, *Minnehaha*, Marble (Metropolitan Museum of Art, 1868), one of several pieces based on Henry Wadsworth Longfellow's epic poem, *The Song of Hiawatha*.

Abraham Lincoln delivering his second inaugural address, Washington, DC, March 4, 1865.

In the years after she created her dying Cleopatra, both the artist and her masterpiece were lost to history. But now we know that Ms. Lewis ended her days in England, in 1907. Her Cleopatra wound up in Washington DC.

But there's a little more to tell.

About the time Ms. Lewis left for Italy, President Abraham Lincoln's 2nd Inaugural Ball was held, March 6, 1865, at the old Patent Office Building when it was new. Little did he know that, in about five weeks, he'd be mortally wounded over at Ford's Theatre. Or that the building where he and his wife were dancing would be a treasure house of art, including a dying queen sculpted by a great African American artist.

Find Out More

READ: *Child of the Fire: Mary Edmonia Lewis and the Problem of Art History's Black and Indian Subject* by Kirsten Pai Buick

VISIT: americanart.si.edu/collections/search/artist/?id=2914

Franz Liszt

An Inspiration for Musical Mania

BY JIM WHITING

The word mania refers to feelings of frenzy, increased physical activity, and an especially good mood. So when four mop-haired musicians from Liverpool, England were taking the world by storm in 1963, Canadian music writer Sandy Gardiner thought it was the perfect term to describe the effect they had on audiences: "A new disease is sweeping through Britain, Europe, and the Far East...and doctors are powerless to stop it. Its name is—BEATLEMANIA!"

Im Concertsaale!

A Liszt concert often created a sensation.

Portrait of Franz Liszt by Henri Lehmann, 1839.

The following year, Beatlemania came to the United States when George Harrison, John Lennon, Paul McCartney, and Ringo Starr performed on the Ed Sullivan Show, a popular television program. During the show and the live concerts that followed, members of the audience—largely teenage girls—screamed and shrieked.

The Beatles weren't the first musicians to inspire a mania. That honor belongs to nineteenth-century Hungarian pianist Franz Liszt, whom many music historians call the world's first rock star for his scintillating performances in solo recitals. The frenzy he induced in his audiences prompted the German poet Heinrich Heine to coin the term "Lisztomania" in 1844. Liszt enjoyed many of the same perks as the Beatles: hero worship, adoring groupies, hobnobbing with royalty, widespread media coverage, and more.

Liszt was very handsome and fully aware of his good looks. Everything he did on stage was calculated to produce the maximum dramatic effect. As his fingers

Photo of Franz Liszt by Franz Hanfstaengl, circa 1860.

rippled over the piano keys, he flung his head from side to side as his shoulder-length hair cascaded around his face. He was so energetic that globs of sweat sometimes sprayed the front rows.

His audience—mainly women in their 20s, 30s and 40s—totally bought into his act. Like Beatles spectators, they screamed at dramatic spots in the recital. Often they went further. As the last notes of the concert rang out, many rushed the stage in their zeal to obtain a souvenir. Almost anything would do—a piece of his clothing, strands of his hair, broken piano strings, the fabric of the chair he had sat on. They especially wanted the still-damp handkerchiefs Liszt used to wipe his face. Perhaps the ultimate prizes were his discarded cigar butts. Women lucky enough to snatch one would light it and thereby gain quite literally a taste of their hero.

There's a tangible connection between the two manias. They both inspired movies—*A Hard Day's Night* (1964) for the Beatles and Ken Russell's *Lisztomania* eleven years later. In the Russell film, the role of the Pope is played by Ringo Starr!

Find Out More

READ: *Franz Liszt* by Jim Whiting

LISTEN: to Franz Liszt's music at youtube.com/watch?v= KpOtuoHL45Y

WATCH: Hungarian Rhapsody #2, youtube.com/watch?v= scjBYNxDCDA

Robert Morris

Abolitionist and Attorney

BY DOREEN RAPPAPORT

Seven white guards ringed the courtroom. Two more stood at Shadrach Minkins' side. His lawyer Robert Morris, a black member of the Boston Vigilance Committee—a group of abolitionists who helped runaway slaves like Minkins—talked softly to him. Five other white men who were also abolitionists stood behind Morris. Shadrach appreciated their support, but he knew it wouldn't matter. His three months of freedom in Boston, Massachusetts were over; he would be dragged back to Norfolk, Virginia and his owner, John DeBree. The Fugitive Slave Act of 1850 had been passed a year earlier: If runaway slaves were tracked

SALES THIS DAY.

PURSUANT to an advertisement affixed to the door of the Court House of the city of Norfolk,

WILL BE SOLD,

At Public Auction, before the Court House, at 12 o'-clock, on MONDAY, the 23d inst.,

Negro Man Shadrach and Negro Woman Hester and her children Jim and Imogene, by virtue of a writ of fieri facias against the goods and chattels of Martha Hutchings and Edward DeCormis, at suit of Joseph Cowperthwaite, assignee of the President, Directors & Co. of the Bank of the United States.

jy 18—tds   WM. B. LAMB, Serg't.
(Beacon copy.)

An 1849 ad offering Shadrach Minkins for sale in Norfolk, VA.

Admitted to the Massachusetts bar in 1847, Robert Morris may have been the first black male lawyer to file a lawsuit in the United States.

down in the free states, they had to be returned to their owners.

The guards started letting a few people at a time into the courtroom until it was packed with over 150 black men and about fifty white men.

Morris went up with DeBree's lawyer to speak to the judge.

"I need more time to prepare my client's case," Morris told the judge.

Debree's lawyer protested. The judge agreed to give Morris a few more days. Then he ordered the courtroom cleared. Most of the white men hurried out. Not one black man moved.

An April 24, 1851 poster warning the "colored people of Boston" about policemen acting as slave catchers, pursuant to the Fugitive Slave Law of 1850.

"Clear the court!" the bailiff shouted.

No one moved.

The guards walked threateningly toward the black spectators, and they reluctantly got up to leave. The guard opened the courtroom door just wide enough for one man at a time to exit. Shadrach watched them leave. Morris was the last. When the door was opened for him, twenty black men and a good number of whites pushed into the courtroom.

The guards on either side of Shadrach pressed him close. The seven guards along the wall tried to move toward Shadrach, but the crowd moved more quickly and pressed them back. Two men hoisted Shadrach to his feet. "Take him out the side door," someone shouted.

A guard's voice echoed in Shadrach's ears as the crowd ran triumphantly out the side courtroom door, down the stairs, out into the street with their prize.

Five days later, on February 20, 1851, Shadrach arrived in Canada shepherded by various Underground Railroad conductors along the way. His rescue caused an uproar. Southerners demanded an investigation. Northern abolitionists insisted the Fugitive Slave Act was illegal. Eight men, including Morris were arrested, but the charges were dropped.

Eighteen months later Shadrach was married and running a barber shop in Montreal.

FIND OUT MORE

READ: *Escape from Slavery: Five Journeys to Freedom* by Doreen Rappaport

READ: *No More! Stories of Slave Resistance* by Doreen Rappaport, illustrated by Shane Evans

VISIT: masshist.org/longroad/01slavery/minkins.htm.

Rosa Parks

The Mother of the Civil Rights Movement

BY JIM WHITING

When seamstress Rosa Parks boarded a bus after work in Montgomery, Alabama on December 1, 1955, she had no idea she was about to make history.

At that time, Montgomery buses were strictly segregated. According to city law, whites had the right to the first few rows of seats. Under a long-standing custom, blacks had to give up their seats as additional whites boarded. So when that happened,

The restored bus that Rosa Parks sat in on December 1, 1955 was on exhibit in Washington, D.C.'s National Mall for the 50th Anniversary of the March on Washington.

the driver ordered Parks and three other blacks to move further back. The other three did. Parks didn't. The driver repeated his order. Again Parks refused. She was arrested.

Years later, a legend spread that she was tired from a long day on her feet. But as she explained, "No, the only tired I was, was tired of giving in."

Black leaders, who had long shared her frustration, sensed an opportunity. They quickly formed the Montgomery Improvement Association (MIA) and selected a young minister who had just moved to Montgomery as leader. His name was Dr. Martin Luther King, Jr.

Rosa Parks being fingerprinted.

Left: Rosa Parks' Montgomery Bus Boycott mug shot. Right: Rosa Parks in 1955. Do you recognize the man in the background?

Under his leadership, Montgomery blacks ordered a boycott of the bus system. They used many methods of alternate transportation, sometimes walking for an hour or even more. Despite whites' burning of several churches and an explosion that destroyed Dr. King's home, they persisted: day after day, week after week, month after month. Since blacks formed about 75 percent of the normal ridership, the loss of their fares began crippling the system. Finally, on December 20 the following year Montgomery repealed the law requiring segregated buses. The victory also catapulted Dr. King to national prominence.

Parks didn't fare so well. She was fired from her job and received numerous death threats. She and her husband moved to Detroit.

Honors began pouring in. In 2000, *Time* magazine named Rosa Parks—often called the "Mother of the Civil Rights Movement"—as one of the 100 most important people of the twentieth century.

President Barack Obama sits in the famous Rosa Parks bus at the Henry Ford Museum after an event in Dearborn, Michigan.

Parks had another honor that year. In 1994, the white supremacist group Ku Klux Klan had announced a plan to clean up a portion of Highway I-55 near St. Louis, Missouri under the federal Adopt-a-Highway program. That meant signs would be posted to acknowledge the Klan's "public service." The Missouri Department of Transportation objected, but a series of court cases concluding in 2000 deemed the objection as unconstitutional. The state quickly responded by naming that portion of I-55 the Rosa Parks Freeway. The Klan never did clean it up.

Find Out More

READ: *Rosa Parks* by Jim Whiting

VISIT: history.com/topics/black-history/rosa-parks

Radium Girls

The Taste of Death

BY CARLA KILLOUGH MCCLAFFERTY

Radium is a radioactive element that glows. In the early decades of the twentieth century, companies such as the U.S. Radium Corporation made money from this unusual characteristic. They manufactured watches that were painted with radium paint that allowed users to tell time in the dark.

The employees hired to paint the tiny numbers and hands of watch faces were mostly young immigrant women. It was a good job with better-than-average pay. Also, it was exciting to work with the world-famous radium. Just for fun sometimes the girls would paint radium on their teeth or fingernails to show their boyfriends how they glowed in the dark. After all, the company told the girls that radium was harmless.

Each girl painted the faces of 250 to 300 watch dials in a typical workday. To do this delicate work, it took

a steady hand and a pointed paint brush. Throughout the day, in order to keep a sharp point on their brushes, the girls would put the tip between their lips then dip it into the radium paint.

An early twentieth-century clock with radium numbers and hands.

97

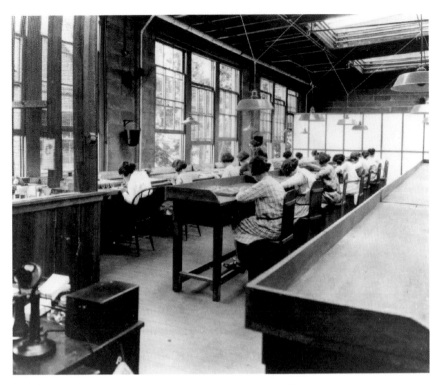

Radium girls painting watch dials at a U.S. Radium Corporation factory, 1922.

In 1921 Amelia Maggia, one of the dial painters, had a swollen cheek and terrible toothache. She had the tooth pulled but her gums would not heal. Infection set in and destroyed her jawbone. She died the next year from her mysterious condition. Then another young woman developed the same symptoms. Then another. Then another. Each of the girls had one thing in common: they were radium dial painters. Ultimately they learned that every time they put their brushes to their mouths, their bodies absorbed radium, and that radiation was harmful to people.

In 1928, five "radium girls" sued U.S. Radium Corporation. By the time the case went to trial each woman was dying from radium poisoning. One of the girls, Grace Fryer, had so much radium in her system that when she blew her nose, the handkerchief glowed in the dark. The company decided to settle the case, and agreed to pay their medical bills and give them

A 1918 ad for the first products to use "Actual Radium, an astonishing new force for betterment, applied as an aid to Beauty."

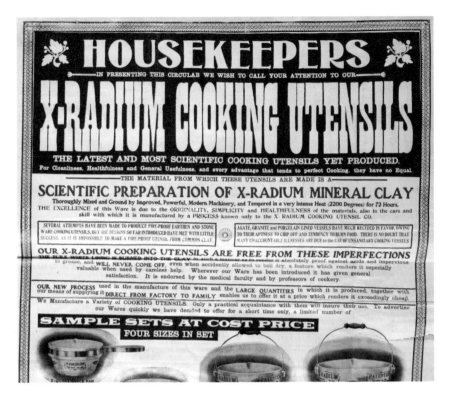

A 1905 ad for "X-radium cooking utensils. The latest and most scientific cooking utensils yet produced."

each a one-time lump sum of $10,000, plus $600 per year for the rest of their lives—which weren't very long. Sadly, it took the deaths of the "radium girls" and many others to understand the dangers of radium.

Find Out More

READ: *Something Out of Nothing: Marie Curie and Radium* by Carla Killough McClafferty

VISIT: Official site of Nobel Prize Laureates, Marie Curie: nobelprize.org/nobel_prizes/physics/laureates/1903/marie-curie-bio.html

VISIT: npr.org/2014/12/28/373510029/saved-by-a-bad-taste-one-of-the-last-radium-girls-dies-at-107

Sally Ride

"Ride, Sally, Ride!"

BY JIM WHITING

In 1983, shortly before she became America's first female astronaut to participate in a mission, Sally Ride faced a press conference. Reporters raised questions they would never have asked a man: "Will the flight affect your reproductive organs?" one inquired. "Do you weep when things go wrong on the job?" queried another. A third wondered, "Will you wear makeup and a bra in space?" *Tonight Show* host Johnny Carson

As one of the three mission specialists on the STS-7 mission, Ride played a vital role. In this image, Dr. Ride sits in the aft flight deck mission specialist's seat during deorbit preparations.

First *Challenger* launch on April 4, 1983.

On June 18, 1983, Sally Ride became the first American woman in space as a crew member on space shuttle *Challenger*. Here she communicates with ground controllers from the flight deck during the six-day mission.

joked that the flight was delayed because Sally had to find a purse that matched her shoes.

It wasn't just US media. The Soviet Union had already sent two women into space. When one of them arrived at the space station, a male cosmonaut (the Soviet term for astronauts) said, "An apron is waiting for you in the kitchen."

By this point, Sally had mastered parachute jumping, water survival, coping with weightlessness and the massive G-forces from a rocket launch, and other highly demanding skills. She flew jet planes. She had a PhD degree in physics from Stanford, one of the nation's top universities. She helped develop a robotic arm for use on the space shuttle. She was a nationally ranked tennis player who decided not to turn pro because she preferred science.

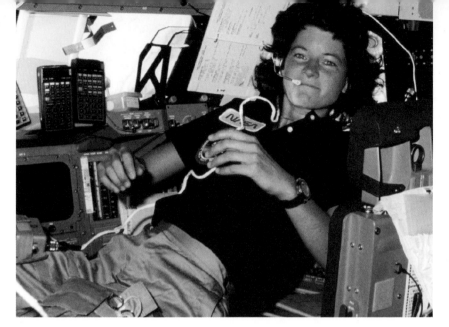

Ride, shown here floating in the *Challenger* flight deck, later described the launch as "exhilarating, terrifying and overwhelming all at the same time."

The general public seemed more accepting. On launch day at Florida's Cape Canaveral, thousands of people wore "Ride, Sally, Ride!" T-shirts, from the lyrics of the pop song "Mustang Sally."

The mission went flawlessly, and Sally flew again the following year. She was scheduled for a third flight in 1986, but it was scrubbed when the *Challenger* space shuttle blew up.

Sally left the space program soon afterward. She was passionate about encouraging young people—especially girls—to become involved in STEM (Science, Technology, Engineering, Math). Here are some of the things she did toward that achieving that goal:

- She originated the Sally Ride EarthKAM project, in which middle school students request that astronauts take photos of any point on Earth. Students research features in the images to provide additional material for subjects they are studying.

On June 18, 1983, one of Sally Ride's jobs was to call out "Roll program," seven seconds after launch. "I'll guarantee that those were the hardest words I ever had to get out of my mouth," she said later.

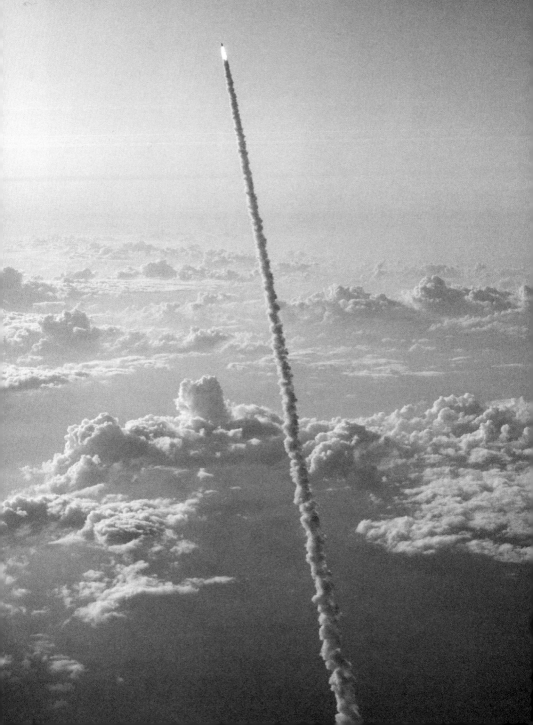

Sally Ride Science Festivals continue to bring hundreds of students together in day-long celebrations of science.

- Her company Sally Ride Science offers programs encouraging STEM studies.
- Sally Ride Science Festivals bring hundreds of students together in day-long celebrations of science.
- She wrote seven children's books about the Earth and various aspects of space travel.

Sadly, Sally Ride died of cancer in 2012 at the age of 61. Shortly afterward, President Barack Obama awarded her the Presidential Medal of Freedom. It is the nation's highest civilian honor.

Find Out More

READ: *Sally Ride: A Photobiography of America's Pioneering Woman in Space* by Tam O'Shaughnessy

VISIT: sallyridescience.com/about/sallyride

Cal Rodgers

A Transcontinental First

BY ROXIE MUNRO

You've probably heard about Charles Lindberg, the first pilot to fly across the Atlantic. But have you ever heard of Cal Rodgers?

Only eight years after the Wright brothers flew the first heavier-than-air machine, newspaper tycoon William Hearst offered a $50,000 prize to the first to fly across the continent in less than 30 days.

Although Cal Rodgers had just learned to fly, he was ready. "He'll need every atom of courage," Wilbur Wright had said of any man who attempted to win the prize.

The nation had not a single airport, and there were no navigation aids or repair places. To help him, a train carrying a second plane, spare parts, a crew of mechanics, Cal's wife, Mabel, his mother, and reporters was rented by a company producing a grape drink named Vin Fiz. In exchange, Cal named his airplane after it, and would scatter Vin Fiz promotional leaflets from the sky—the first aerial ad campaign.

On September 17, 1911, Cal took off from Brooklyn, made a sweep over Manhattan and headed for New Jersey, where the train—and an enormous crowd—were waiting.

The next morning, right after takeoff he tried to avoid some power lines, hit a tree, and plunged into a chicken coop. Feathers floated as he emerged from a tangle of wires, splintered wood, and torn fabric. Head bleeding, cigar clenched between his teeth, he muttered, "Oh, my beautiful airplane."

The Vin Fiz departing New York.

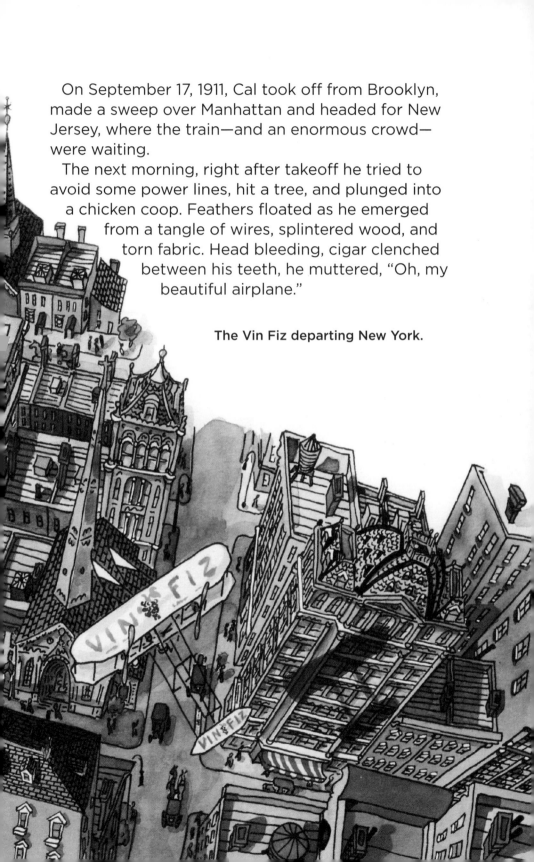

The first of what would be many crashes of the Vin Fiz.

They rebuilt the Vin Fiz, and a few days later, he was again airborne. Stopovers were frequent, as were brushes with death. The plane struck telegraph wires. It piled into a barbed-wire fence (demolished again). After landing in Indiana, Cal was attacked by a bull. He became the first pilot to fly in a thunderstorm. But the Vin Fiz buzzed on.

When he reached Chicago, other contenders had dropped out. Cal realized that he wasn't going to make it to the West Coast in 30 days. But he pressed on.

To avoid the Rocky Mountains, he flew south over Texas, then west. By the time he reached California, after a dozen crashes, his plane had been rebuilt so often that little remained of the original.

A month later, after still another crash and in yet another rebuilt plane, he finally reached the Pacific, greeted by 50,000 spectators

Tragically, Cal's luck ran out. A few months later, he flew into a flock of seagulls, and plunged to his death.

But he did it: He became the first pilot to fly across the American continent.

Find Out More

READ: *Feathers, Flaps, & Flops: Fabulous Early Fliers* by Bo Zaunders, illustrated by Roxie Munro

VISIT: anb.org/articles/20/20-01946.html

Victorious Cal welcomed by his fans and the press. Note the crutches. It was not an easy trip!

Roald Amudsen was a popular and much-admired figure in his time. Roald Dahl, who wrote *Charlie and the Chocolate Factory* and *James and the Giant Peach*, was named after him.

Scott and Amundsen

Race to the Ends of the Earth

BY JIM WHITING

In the early 1900s, becoming the first to reach the South Pole was a huge source of individual and national pride. English explorer Ernest Shackleton came within 97 miles of that goal in 1909 before being forced to turn back.

Fellow Englishman Robert Scott made well-publicized plans to succeed where Shackleton had failed. He was therefore dismayed to learn that Norwegian Roald Amundsen had his own secret plan to reach the Pole. Amundsen hadn't even told his crew members where they were going until they were at sea.

The British National Antarctic Expedition (1901–04) was known as the Discovery Expedition. It was organized jointly by the Royal Society and Royal Geographical Society.

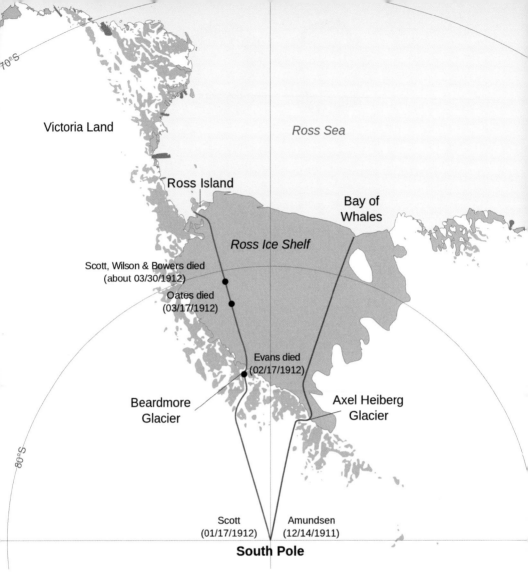

Victoria Land

Ross Sea

Ross Island

Bay of Whales

Ross Ice Shelf

Scott, Wilson & Bowers died
(about 03/30/1912)

Oates died
(03/17/1912)

Evans died
(02/17/1912)

Beardmore
Glacier

Axel Heiberg
Glacier

Scott
(01/17/1912)

Amundsen
(12/14/1911)

South Pole

70°S

80°S

Map showing the polar journeys of Scott's expedition (green) and Amundsen's expedition (red) to reach the South Pole.

The two expeditions landed in Antarctica at roughly the same time and spent months preparing for their respective treks. Amundsen departed on October 18, 1911. He was fortunate to encounter relatively good weather. On December 7, he passed the southernmost point Shackleton had reached. One week later, on December 14, he and his four men stood on the South Pole. Each man grasped the

Robert Scott lacked Amudsen's flair as well as his luck.

Scott's group took this photograph of themselves using a string to operate the shutter on January 17, 1912, the day after they discovered Amundsen had reached the pole first.

Norwegian flag. They celebrated in the evening with seal meat and cigars. Before returning, they erected a tent and put letters for Scott and Norwegian King Haakon inside. Amundsen and his men arrived back at their starting point in late January and sailed to Tasmania, where Amundsen sent a cable trumpeting his accomplishment. Even though the response was mostly favorable, some people in England thought Amundsen had played a dirty trick by being so secretive about his plans.

Meanwhile, Scott and his four men left from their base three weeks after Amundsen. They encountered some of the worst weather Antarctica could throw at them. Several times they had to stay in their tents for extended periods, eating valuable food. They finally arrived at the Pole on January 17, only to have their triumph replaced with bitter disappointment. They found Amundsen's letters and knew they were five weeks too late.

Their difficulties worsened on the way back. Two men died from cold, hunger, and exhaustion. Scott and the two others made what proved to be their final camp on March 19, confined to their tent by horrific weather. They were about 10 miles from a food depot that would have ensured their survival, but couldn't reach it. Searchers found their frozen bodies eight months later.

Amundsen died in 1928 in a plane crash during a rescue mission in the Arctic Ocean. Shortly before his death, he told a journalist, "If only you knew how splendid it is up here, that's where I want to die."

Find Out More

READ: *History Chapters: Roald Amundsen and Robert Scott Race to the South Pole* by Gare Thompson

VISIT: Scott's Last Expedition: Journey to the South Pole, scottslastexpedition.org/expedition/journey-to-the-south-pole

The Observation Hill cross, erected in 1913 as a memorial to Scott and his party.

Mary Shelley

The Woman Makes a Monster

BY CHERYL HARNESS

You know how it is. Old campfire stories, interesting things you're doing or seeing or hearing about—they get all mixed up in your dreams and your stories. That's how it was for Mary Wollstonecraft Godwin. One night in 1816, in Switzerland, when there wasn't anything on TV (because it wasn't invented yet), she and her friends decided they'd each write a horror story. By combining her knowledge with the idea of "what if," 18-year-old Mary made up a story about a monster. It'd turn out to be one of the most famous monsters ever.

These were some of the ideas that influenced Mary's thinking:

- She'd read the Greek mythological story of Prometheus, who got in bad trouble with the gods for stealing their powerful, amazing fire. In fact, Mary's dreamy poet boyfriend, Percy Shelley, whom she'd marry later on, was writing

Above: Reginald Easton painted this miniature portrait of Mary Shelley on ivory.
Left: Illustration from the 1831 edition of *Frankenstein*.

Nearly two hundred years after Mary Shelley created Dr. Frankenstein, the murderous creature the scientist released from his lab still roams through books and appears regularly in movies.

about Prometheus. Their handsome poet-friend George Gordon, known as Lord Byron, had been writing about him too. What if Mary wrote about a scientist who stole God's power of making life?

- People had been talking about this Italian scientist, Luigi Galvani, who'd been doing exciting experiments with electrical sparks. They made animals' muscles move—even if they were dead!
- In her travels in Germany, Mary had seen the medieval Castle Frankenstein.

Hmmm...I'll bet you can guess now what story Mary wrote! In it, her character, Dr. Victor Frankenstein, gathered parts of dead people's bodies in his laboratory. His experiment? He'd make a perfect person then bring it to life with the power of lightning—and it worked! But—oh no! Dr. Frankenstein accidentally created a monster! And then a lot of horrible things happened!

Mary Shelley's Frankenstein, which was first published in 1818, never got very good reviews, but never mind. In the almost two centuries since she wrote it, Mary's monster story has sparked the imaginations of playwrights, moviemakers, cartoonists, musicians, and Halloween costume-makers again and again and again.

It kind of makes you wonder about your own ideas and memories. What if you put them together in your imagination? You could spark a story into life!

Find Out More

READ: *Strange Creatures: The Story of Mary Shelley* by Catherine Wells

VISIT: The Poetry Foundation, poetryfoundation.org/poems-and-poets/poets/detail/mary-wollstonecraft-shelley

Vincent van Gogh

The Case of the Severed Ear

BY JAN GREENBERG

Who was Vincent van Gogh? Ask around and most people come up with the same answer. He was the famous artist who cut off his ear. What is the truth about Vincent van Gogh? Was he a great painter because he led a life of extremes? Or was he a great painter despite his disordered life?

Several years before his death, he began to experience seizures and blackouts during which he heard voices and behaved strangely. Are the pulsating spirals, undulating lines, and dizzying stars of his late paintings what he saw when he was having an attack? Or are they the result of a style he developed painstakingly through years of hard work?

In 1888, Vincent moved to Arles in the south of France. He planned to establish an artists' commune where his friends could live together to create a new direction in painting. Vincent persuaded the artist Paul Gauguin, who was desperate for money, to move to Arles to help him. Vincent also was lonely.

For two months Gauguin lived in the Yellow House Vincent had lovingly filled with paintings hoping to impress his friend. Gauguin bossed Vincent around and criticized his artwork. Eventually, when Gauguin sold a few paintings, he threatened to abandon Vincent.

Finally, on Christmas Eve, after a quarrel at dinner,

Vincent van Gogh, *The Yellow House*, oil on canvas, 1888. This is the house at 2 Place Lamartine, Arles, France, where, on May 1, 1888, Vincent van Gogh rented four rooms and where Paul Gauguin lived for nine weeks from late October, 1888. The left wing housed a grocery. Van Gogh indicated that the restaurant, where he used to have his meals, was in the building painted pink close to the left edge of the painting.

Gauguin stalked off into the streets. Vincent followed him. What happened next is unclear, but Vincent returned to the Yellow House alone and cut off his earlobe (not the whole ear) with a razor. Vincent couldn't remember the details of this terrible night. But when he was discharged from the hospital a few weeks later, he went right back to work.

There have been many theories about Vincent's condition. The theory most generally accepted is that

Left: Vincent van Gogh, *Self-portrait with Bandaged Ear*, 1889. Right: *Self-portrait* by Paul Gauguin, 1885.

he suffered from epilepsy, a disease that could have caused his seizures and hallucinations and for which there was no medication. In Vincent's case, another reason for his "attacks" might have been his habit of drinking absinthe, an alcoholic drink popular in nineteenth-century France. It contains a strong nerve poison, now illegal in most countries.

Today many popular performers advertise how dangerous and extreme their lives are by writing shocking lyrics and acted outrageously on stage. They are mimicking the lives of artists such as Van Gogh. But he was not advertising or pretending. He just wanted to be useful—to make art that would last. His glorious paintings are the result of his discipline and dedication, despite the turmoil of his life.

Find Out More

READ: *Vincent Van Gogh: Portrait of an Artist* by Jan Greenberg and Sandra Jordan

VISIT: vangoghgallery.com

Queen Victoria and Albert

The Quest for a Happy Marriage

BY ANDREA WARREN

When eighteen-year-old Victoria was crowned queen of England in 1837, the British wondered and worried who their very young queen would marry. Whoever he was, he would have power and influence, so the queen's choice was critical.

Victoria had many royal suitors and was getting advice from all directions about which alliance with which suitor would be most advantageous for England. But as the British quickly learned, their new queen had a mind of her own, and she had already

**Left: Coronation portrait of Queen Victoria by George Hayter.
Right: Portrait of Prince Albert by John Partridge, 1840.**

The Marriage of Victoria by George Hayter. It has been said that Queen Victoria started the bridal custom of wearing a white wedding gown.

picked Prince Albert of Saxe-Coburg, an area of what is now Bavaria, Germany.

The British were shocked! Royalty often intermarried, so it wasn't because Victoria and Albert were first cousins (her mother and his father were sister and brother), but because there was a great deal of anti-German sentiment in England at the time. Victoria didn't care. He was her "dear Albert," and they were married in 1840 when they were both twenty-one. They loved each other and were determined that theirs would be a happy marriage.

The odds were against this. Neither Albert nor Victoria had grown up in happy families. In fact, both had been exposed to mostly miserable marriages. Victoria was spoiled, stubborn, and had a quick temper. Fortunately, Albert was a kind man who understood her well and knew how to be patient with her. That patience was put to the test many times as they raised their nine children. Victoria disliked being pregnant and wasn't fond of babies and toddlers. But Albert provided balance. He doted on their four sons and five daughters and was closely involved in their care and education.

The British public adored the royal family, and they came to love the scholarly Albert. He became a British citizen, was a wise political advisor to Victoria, and was active in public life. When he died from stomach problems in 1861 at age forty-two, the British grieved for him.

Victoria went into deep mourning. Often called "the widow of Windsor," she wore only black and lived a secluded life at Windsor Castle until her own death at age eighty-one. Today, her name and Albert's grace London's great Victoria and Albert Museum, known affectionately as the V&A. London is also home to several major public monuments that were commissioned by Victoria to honor her "dear Albert" and which serve as a reminder that theirs was truly a royal love story.

Find Out More

READ: *Charles Dickens and the Street Children of London* by Andrea Warren.

VISIT: historic-uk.com/HistoryUK/HistoryofBritain/Queen-Victoria

Albert, Victoria and their nine children, 1857. Left to right: Alice, Arthur, Albert, Edward, Leopold, Louise, Victoria with Beatrice, Alfred, Victoria, and Helena.

Malala has lived by her own words: "When the whole world is silent, even one voice becomes powerful."

Malala Yousafzai

Motivation and Inspiration

BY VICKI COBB

Just the thought of Malala Yousafzai brings tears to my eyes. If you don't know who she is, you should. At the age of seventeen, she was the youngest person to ever receive the Nobel Peace Prize.

From the time she was eleven, she had a single purpose: to fight for the right to an education for every girl and boy on the planet. As a Pakistani, where women live life in the shadows, she faced many obstacles in expressing her beliefs. In October of 2012, when she was fifteen, she was shot in the head on her school bus—the target of assassination. The Taliban claimed credit for this diabolical act. Miraculously, she survived without serious impairment. But the brutality of the Taliban did not stop her; neither did an earthquake, a flood, or the lack of financial resources. She continued to speak out on behalf of education for all.

I've recently read her memoir, *I Am Malala*. She is like the child in the fable "The Emperor's New Clothes," who speaks unvarnished truth with the impeccable logic of the child who does not understand political correctness.

"If they [the Taliban] come, what would you do Malala? . . ." she writes. "If you hit a Talib with your shoe, then there will be no difference between you and the Talib. You must not treat others . . . with cruelty . . . you must fight others but through peace, through

Malala shares some quality time with the Obama family.

dialogue, and through education . . . then I'll tell [the Talib] how important education is and that I even want education for your children as well . . . that's what I want to tell you, now do what you want."

Like *The Diary of Ann Frank*, you cannot escape the voice of a young girl who cares about her hopes and dreams for her future and that of the troubled world.

"I speak not for myself but for those without voice," she writes, "those who have fought for their rights . . . their right to live in peace, their right to be treated with dignity, their right to equality of opportunity, their right to be educated."

How can we motivate students to fight for their own interests in acquiring an education? How can we inspire them to do the hard work needed? Maybe they need to hear Malala speak.

In the United States, we have both the right and the availability to education, yet so many kids don't take advantage of it to make something of themselves. What lesson can we all take away from Malala?

Find Out More

READ: *I Am Malala: How One Girl Stood Up for Education and Changed the World* by Malala Yousafzai with Patricia McCormick

VISIT: brainyquote.com/quotes/authors/m/malala_yousafzai.html

Malala Yousafzai at Women of the World Festival, 2014.

ABOUT THE AUTHORS

JAN ADKINS

Home base: Gainesville, FL
Email: j.adkins@verizon.net
Website: presently being rebuilt at janadkins.com

"All the good stories are real. How could we make up Vlad Dracula? Or Stephen Hawking?"

JAN ADKINS was a distracted, lackadaisical student and understands daydreamers in class. He has written and illustrated more than 40 books on widely different subjects, most of them nonfiction, and feels a special kinship with young readers.

For nine years, he was associate art director at *National Geographic Magazine*. He taught illustration at Rhode Island School of Design and at Maryland Institute College of Art. He's a sailor and a cook, a hunter and a builder, and most of all, a delighted grandfather. He now hikes and bicycles and canoes around Gainesville, Florida.

*You might enjoy Jan Adkin's trilogy—*What If You Met a Pirate, What If You Met a Knight, *and* What If You Met a Cowboy*—about historical figures who are not what movies show. His book* Bridges: From My Side to Yours, *is a history of engineering over human history told through bridges. He is just finishing a new book,* Bertha Takes a Drive, *about Bertha Benz taking the first road trip in the first automobile, defying church and state and, technically, committing the first grand theft auto. What a girl that Bertha was!*

SARAH ALBEE

Home base: Watertown, CT
Email: albees@taftschool.org
Website: www.sarahalbeebooks.com

"My books are a mash-up of history and science. I believe high-interest topics presented with humor and passion can go a long way toward coaxing reluctant readers into appreciating history, science, and, yes, reading books."

 SARAH ALBEE is the *New York Times* bestselling author of more than 100 books for kids, ranging from preschool through middle grade.

She played basketball in college, and then a year of semi-professional women's basketball in Cairo, Egypt. Prior to being a full-time writer, Sarah worked at Children's Television Workshop (the producers of *Sesame Street*) for nine years. She lives in Connecticut with her husband, who is a high school history teacher and administrator, their three kids, and their dog, Rosie.

As a visiting author, Sarah keeps kids engaged through active participation, funny props, and amazing visuals, and helps them make connections between their own lives and what happened in history. She also loves to help them with crafting their own writing.

Sarah's mission is to get kids to see how awesome history can be. She does this by choosing topics that interest and amuse them, for example Poop Happened! A History of What People Do with Their Waste; *or* Bugged: How Insects Changed History, *a look at the world through fly-specked glasses; or* Why'd They Wear That?, *which describes the funky, disgusting, regrettable, and life-threatening creations people have worn throughout the course of human history.*

VICKI COBB

Home base: Greenburgh, NY
Email: email@vickicobb.com
Website: www.vickicobb.com
Blogs: www.nonfictionminute.org,
     www.huffingtonpost.com/vicki-cobb

"All of my work is dedicated to giving the joy of discovery

to children, which creates the foundation for a lifetime of ongoing inquiry and learning."

 VICKI COBB, the "Julia Child" of kids' hands-on science, was born in New York City where she attended a private progressive school in Greenwich Village from kindergarten to sixth grade. She loved school because they were always creating new things, reading great books and doing projects. When she was 12, her family moved to Tarrytown, NY, and she attended a traditional public school. It was not nearly as much fun so instead of continuing to eleventh grade, she went to college. That was better, but it still wasn't as much fun as elementary school. However, she did become very interested in science. Her first jobs after graduating were in lab research. They involved doing the same things over and over again. So she went back to school to become a science teacher.

Teaching was a blast! But, she decided that the thing she enjoyed most was writing science books for children. Looking back, after 90+ books, she realizes that she's made her life's work creating elementary school for herself so she would never stop having fun!

Vicki Cobb's classic book, Science Experiments You Can Eat *was released bigger and better than ever in 2016. Her five most fun books that are quick bets about science are now in one huge book:* We Dare You! *You can see the videos at www.wedareyouvideos.com. You might also check out her DK biographies on Marie Curie and Harry Houdini.*

JAN GREENBERG

Home base: St. Louis, MO
Email: jngreenb@aol.com
Website: jangreenbergsandrajordan.com

"My goal has been to help young readers come to new art with a fresh and open mind and to begin a conversation that will continue throughout their lives."

JAN GREENBERG was born in St. Louis, Missouri. She still lives there with her husband Ronnie and their two brown standard poodles, Henri and Diego. When their three daughters grew up and left home, she was done with writing about teenagers and their woes. No more inspiration! She decided to stretch her brain in a new direction. She lives in a rambling old house filled with artworks, many of them abstract or very large, such as a ten-foot pink balloon rabbit made of Plexiglas. Her daughters' friends would come over and ask questions, such as "Do your parents really like that stuff?" or "Is that supposed to be art?" After some research she discovered there were no books for young readers about contemporary American art. It was a gap in the bookshelf waiting to be filled.

Since 1991, she has been working on books about the arts, many of them with Sandra Jordan. They spend a lot of time in museums, artists' studios, and sculpture parks, looking at art, interviewing American artists and architects, and talking, talking, talking. She is interested in poems about artwork (*Heart to Heart* and *Side by Side*), new architecture (*Frank O. Gehry Outside In*), dance (*Ballet for Martha*), artists (*Cindy Sherman*), and anything to do with new art and new ways to make it. When she is not working on a book, she is hiking in Colorado with girlfriends, daughters, grandchildren, and her dogs.

In addition to 22 books of fiction and nonfiction for young readers, Ms. Greenberg has published numerous short stories, and articles.

A partial list of Jan Greenberg's books includes Action Jackson *(with Sandra Jordan);* Vincent Van Gogh: Portrait of an Artist *(with Sandra Jordan);* Heart to Heart: New Poems Inspired by 20th Century American Art; Ballet for Martha: Making Appalachian Spring *(with Sandra Jordan, Illustrated by Brian Floca); and* The Mad Potter: George E. Ohr Eccentric Genius *(with Sandra Jordan),* Meet Cindy Sherman: Artist, Photogtapher, Chameleon *(with Sandra Jordan), and* Out of the Desert: The Story of the Pintupi Nine, an Aboriginal Australian Family *(with Dennis Scholl).*

CHERYL HARNESS

Home base: Independence, MO
Email: cheryl@cherylharness.com
Website: www.cherylharness.com

"I see my job as countering the notion that history consists of boring factoids about dead people and wars. No, it's a big, fat ongoing drama."

CHERYL HARNESS entered into the world at the time-space intersection of 1951—southern California, but it wasn't long before her restless parents moved back home to western Missouri. Having decided to take Cheryl along on this and lots of other moves, she grew up in a series of book-filled houses thereabouts, with a seemingly endless succession of younger siblings. She read and drew a lot, studied art at the University of Central Missouri and worked as a greeting card artist, unwittingly preparing herself to be an author and/or illustrator of about 50 books. She's talks a lot about them with school kids all over the country, and then goes home to Independence, Missouri, to be with her Shih Tzu, Mimi Squashface Barkymouth, and her cat, Kitty Boy.

There's an awful lot to like, learn, and look at in Cheryl's historical picture books, like *Ghosts of the Civil War, The Remarkable Benjamin Franklin,* and *Remember the Ladies.* She illustrated all three of them.

Cheryl's lively biographies and social histories are noted for their detailed illustrations, researched in her travels round the nation. She and her books help educators teach about the vast panoply of life going on in America from the 1600s to the 1900s.

KERRIE LOGAN HOLLIHAN

Home base: Cincinnati, OH
Email: whollihan@cinci.rr.com
Website: www.kerriehollihan.com

I "tell it like it was." Kids don't get credit for being able to understand history as it plays out. I put the past in context, and I tackle tough topics: segregated America, religious persecution, women's rights, the bleakness of war. I explain the 'whys' as well as the 'whats.' For teens, I deal with young people at turning points in their lives, which helps my readers build links to the past and to young people who felt every bit as modern as today's teens see themselves.

KERRIE LOGAN loves to share her joy in writing with students of all ages. When I meet with middle graders, I ask them to sit quietly for a minute to think. I encourage them to unplug and take time to wonder, just as Isaac Newton did. And I finish my presentations with "What if?.." Hands-on learning helps kids make connections with the past, so I create activities to draw my readers into the lives of people in my books. What's more, narrative nonfiction is an art form! I work to make my words sing.

Among Kerrie's favorite books that she has written are In the Fields and in the Trenches: The Famous and the Forgotten on the Battlefields of World War I, Reporting Under Fire: 16 Daring Women War Correspondents and Photojournalists, Rightfully Ours: How Women Won the Vote, *and* Theodore Roosevelt for Kids—*and she has one coming up on mummies (the kind that are wrapped up in bandages).*

CARLA KILLOUGH MCCLAFFERTY

Home base: Benton, Arkansas
Email: ckmcclafferty@gmail.com
Website: carlamcclafferty.com

"Research is like a treasure hunt. I find fascinating nuggets of information on my subject and use those details to write true stories that are exciting, entertaining, and enjoyable."

CARLA McCLAFFERTY was born in Arkansas and grew up in a tiny, rural community called Tomberlin. Her parents were rice and soybean farmers. Although neither her elementary school nor her hometown had a library, she always loved to read.

Her first career was as a registered radiologic technologist, which she gave up once she began writing nonfiction books for young readers. McClafferty especially loves to write biographies about the lives of "ordinary people who do extraordinary things."

McClafferty shares her award-winning books with audiences of all ages. She provides live author visits with students, professional development workshops with teachers, and interactive videoconferences for both students and teachers on a wide variety of topics.

Read how Carla Killough McClafferty combines fascinating nuggets of information, science, history, art, and medical imaging in her books: Fourth Down and Inches: Concussions and Football's Make-or-Break Moment, The Many Faces of George Washington: Remaking a Presidential Icon, In Defiance of Hitler: The Secret Mission of Varian Fry, *and* Something Out of Nothing: Marie Curie and Radium.

ROXIE MUNRO

Home base: New York, NY
E-mail: roxiesstudio@gmail.com
Website: www.roxiemunro.com

"Nonfiction is more exciting and stimulating than most fiction—we live in an amazing world."

ROXIE MUNRO grew up in southern Maryland, by the Chesapeake Bay. At six, she won first prize in a county-wide contest for a painting of a bowl of fruit, the start of a life-long career as an artist.

In 1980 she moved to New York City, when *The New Yorker* magazine started buying her paintings for covers; she's had fourteen published. In the mid-1980s, Roxie

started writing and illustrating children's books. She's gone on to publish more than forty award-winning nonfiction books, and three interactive "Roxie" apps. Subjects include architecture, nature, biographies, and concepts, like quirky ABC books, mazes, lift-the-flap paper-engineered books, and more, many using "gamification" to engage children. She has also created giant kid-sized stage-set designs for KIWi (Kids Interactive Walk-In) Storybooks, as well as nine apps built to work with them. She loves to take content crossmedia.

Rodent Rascals *(2018) joins Roxie's nature book series on fascinating critters:* Hatch! *(birds),* Busy Builders *(bugs), and* Slithery Snakes*. They all use simple games or concepts to impart information.* EcoMazes: 12 Earth Adventures *and* Market Maze *use mazes to explain ecosystems and where our food comes from. She has a new book about art, called* Masterpiece Mix.

AMY NATHAN

Home base: Larchmont, NY
Email: amynbooks@gmail.com
Website: www.amynathanbooks.com

"The people I've interviewed have inspired me, particularly their determination to follow their dreams, no matter what obstacles may seem to block the way. I hope their stories will inspire the books' readers."

AMY NATHAN grew up in Baltimore, Maryland, and dreamed of being an actress. She also loved to read, especially books about real people and real events. Three books she read as a child made such a strong impression that she remembers them clearly today. They were about people being treated unfairly who stood up for their rights and were helped by others who had the courage to do so. She tried being an actress after college (where she majored in history). But she soon realized that what she liked most about acting was learning about the characters she was portraying, doing research to figure out why they did what they did. She switched from playing people on stage to writing about them—first in articles for Scholastic magazines and then in books for young people. The three books she remembers from her childhood led her to write about other heroes who stood up for their rights, followed their dreams, and helped others—people like Sarah Keys Evans and Marian Anderson. Visit Amy's website for the names of the books from her childhood that inspired her to become a writer (look at the end of the "About the Author" page).

Here are some of Amy's books you might enjoy: Round and Round Together: Taking a Merry-Go-Round Ride into the Civil Rights Movement*, a book about the de-segregation of that Baltimore amusement park, also mentions Marian Anderson;* Yankee Doodle Gals: Women Pilots of World War II*, about the first U.S. women military pilots;* Take a Seat—Make a Stand*, about Sarah Keys Evans;* The Young Musicians' Survival Guide*, about kids with the determination to make beautiful music.*

DOREEN RAPPAPORT

Home base: Copake Falls, New York
Email: rapabook@aol.com
Website: www.doreenrappaport.com

"I want children to understand that they too have the capacity to empower themselves and shape the futures they want. If I have a mission, that's my mission."

DOREEN RAPPAPORT'S life was transformed in the summer of 1965 when she taught in a Freedom school in McComb, Mississippi. There she met "ordinary" people who did extraordinary things. The experience launched her on a career to introduce children to the strivings and struggles of human beings. She has written about "Celebrated"

Americans—Abraham Lincoln, Eleanor Roosevelt, and Martin Luther King, Jr.—and "Not-Yet-Celebrated" Americans—Olaudah Equiano, Zitkala-Sa, and Thecla Mitchell. She spent ten years researching Jewish resisters who fought their oppressors in the nightmare of the Holocaust. Her books have been praised for their meticulous research and varied literary styles.

Doreen's books include Frederick's Journey: The Life of Frederick Douglass, *which won numerous awards and recognitions, including National Council of Social Studies (NCSS), Best Trade Books of the Year; Junior Library Guild; New York Public Library, 100 Books for Reading and Sharing and* Elizabeth Started All the Trouble, *recognitions include Junior Literary Guild; ALA Notable Book; Kirkus Award List; NCSS, Best Trade Books of the Year.*

ANDREA WARREN

Home base: Eastern Kansas
Email: andrea@andreawarren.com
Website: www.andreawarren.com

ANDREA WARREN knows how to have fun, but when she writes she brings to life the true stories of young people in history who have faced enormous challenges and have chosen to live productive lives instead of giving into bitterness. In her eight books she has taken readers into the violence of the Civil War with young Buffalo Bill Cody and with children trying to survive the siege of Vicksburg.

Her readers have found themselves in the orphanages of Vietnam during the war, and even in the Nazi death camps. Readers have hopped aboard the orphan trains with children searching for new homes, they have experienced the hardships of homesteading the Nebraska prairie, and the desperate childhood of Charles Dickens. When she isn't writing, Warren is reading, traveling, attending theatre, and enjoying her friends, children, and grandchildren. She has won many awards and loves to present to children.

For a sampling of her books, she suggests: Orphan Train Rider: One Boy's True Story, Pioneer Girl: A True Story of Growing Up on the Prairie, *and* Charles Dickens and the Street Children of London.

JIM WHITING

Home base: Bainbridge Island, WA
Email: jimruns3@gmail.com
Website: www.jimwhiting.com

"Constantly learning new stuff is one of the main reasons why I keep writing. It's especially exciting to discover human details about cultural icons."

JIM WHITING's Terrific Tidbits:
1. He published *Northwest Runner*, voted by panels of professional journalists as the country's best regional running magazine, for 17 years.
2. He traveled to Antarctica to cover the Antarctica Marathon, although his most vivid memory of the experience is the smell produced by multitudes of pooping penguins.
3. He ran in both the original Olympic stadium, which dates back to 776 BCE (after which he was nearly tossed into the slammer) and the one erected for the revival of the Olympics in 1896.
4. A whale nearly rammed his sailboat *Rachel*. On the way back to the dock, he passed the *Pequod*, another sailboat. (If you've read *Moby Dick,* you'll get the allusions.)
5. He's published nearly 180 nonfiction books for young readers, with another 60 or so in the pipeline. His goal: a stack of books taller than he is (one of the few times he's been glad he's short).

INDEX

Page numbers in **boldface** indicate an illustration.